WITHDRAWN

Living by Faith

BOOKS BY FAITH BALDWIN

FAITH BALDWIN

Living by Faith

Holt, Rinehart and Winston • New York Chicago San Francisco

Some of the material in this volume
has appeared earlier in the Author's monthly
column, "The Open Door," in *Woman's Day*.

First Edition

Designed by Ernst Reichl
80793-1214
Printed in the United States of America

This book is for
Janet Buchanan Hollaman
with love

❧ ❦

"A faithful friend is a strong defense."
THE APOCRYPHA
ECCLESIASTICUS 6:14

Living by Faith

Overture

When the time came to select a title for this little book and the inclusion of the word Faith was suggested, I shied away, thinking that because of my own given name this would imply a rather egotistical pun. However, "Living by Faith," sounds reassuring, whereas "Living *with* Faith"—if we are still relating my name to my book—would be a Herculean task for anyone.

So we'll forget my name and consider faith in its profound and universal sense. The book is, actually, a chronicle of confidence, not self-confidence, but confidence in spiritual values and the guidance of the still, small voice—on the occasions when we listen to it.

As a matter of fact, I think of this stroll through the seasons as a guided tour . . . a tour of the little world around me, the constant alterations of nature, a tour of my thinking, however trivial; a tour of the old house in which I live; and of the more important tour through life itself. I cannot speak for anyone else's life except in general terms common to us all. But that my life-tour, and yours, has been guided I am certain.

In previous books written after the manner of an almanac it amused me to start the year at, if you adhere to a calendar, the

3

wrong time. My first such book began in November; another in October; still another in December. I no longer remember why the first one started in November; the October book came about because October is my birthday month and I always think of birthdays as the beginning of a personal year; as for the journey which began with December, that book had something to do with legacies and gifts, and December is a giving time.

Now I'm starting with November again, and I know why. In that month we have Thanksgiving and I don't know a better way to start a book—or a year, or a day, for that matter—than with thanksgiving.

So much of our thinking directed toward a Higher Power than ourselves is restricted by a framework of pleading, demands, even attempted conciliation and excuses. It rarely flows out and over the barriers of self, into pure gratitude.

Consider the Psalms. Many are pleas for help; many desperate expressions of unhappiness and misery; some a trifle self-laudatory, while others give us rules by which to live righteously. And there are Psalms which importune that one's personal enemies be destroyed and one's own safety be assured. Yet, in many, the clear note of rejoicing is sounded, the song of gratitude and thanksgiving.

It was David who sang: "I will praise Thee, O Lord, with my whole heart; I will shew forth all Thy marvellous works."

And again, "Make a joyful noise unto God, all ye Lands," and, "Oh, sing unto the Lord a new song: sing unto the Lord, all the earth. Sing unto the Lord, bless Hiss name; shew forth His salvation from day to day."

And, "O give thanks unto the Lord, for He is good: for His Mercy endureth for ever."

That is thanksgiving, is it not? So now we start with November. Walk with me through the seasons. Permit me to show you this house, inside and out; upstairs—there are thirteen steps—not very steep, for which I am thankful as my right knee has recently started to plague me. Come with me on my small excursions, watch the weather changes, grow familiar with the birds in the

4

feeders and suffer my rather halting thinking aloud, and the conclusions which are sometimes fairly clear-cut and other times fuzzy around the edges.

And if I repeat myself—and I often do—remember that the passage of the years engrave, and deeply, certain patterns of thought. The remedy here, I suppose, is to try to ignore, if you can't erase, and to break if possible fresh paths, and etch a clearer groove.

Well, if you have remained with me this far, let's begin the tour.

November

Let us go out of the front door—which is, illogically, the side door, but the one we use when we aren't going out of or entering the kitchen—and walk down the worn, gray stone steps and stand a moment on the terrace and look at the three ears of corn, red, black, yellow or mixed, which, if the birds haven't eaten it, hang below the light. If only bare ears, at least the outward sides of them, confront us, I can't help it. In recent years the birds, mainly bluejays, starlings, and blackbirds, have forgotten their manners and consumed the autumnal decor. How they manage this with nothing to perch on—the light's in the way—I haven't the least idea. But it's Thanksgiving time for them as soon as I display the corn.

On the steps—but not where you'll fall over them—and on the terrace are small fat pumpkins; in the little entry hall lovely gourds, yellow, green, and striped, in the pale green Sung bowl, and, throughout the house, small, late-blooming mums; for the bed under the south windows still indulges me with brave blossoms: zinnias, their leaves blackened but the flowers untouched; asters, and the mums.

Now is the season of the final fading leaf, the last to go being oak leaves, pinky brown and tenacious, and days which are often warm before cold nights and the first silent, lazy snowflake drifting down.

Thanksgiving weather, if we aren't engaged in watching snow, reminds me of a loaf of homemade bread—crusty and crisp on the outside, warm and sweet within. For many of our recent Novembers here have been like that, mellow days and frosted nights. This simile may be a little farfetched, but if there's anything better than good home-oven-baked bread I've never eaten it, and anything more pleasant than the last of autumn, smiling her way into winter, I don't know about that either.

But, for a while now, Thanksgiving snowstorms have returned. During a good many years, about forty of them in fact, heavy snows remained just around the corner, peering at us and occasionally contributing a little sparkle, a flash of ice, a few flakes, or a snow shower, just to remind us what—much augmented—would presently be our lot. Yet, when I was a child, Thanksgiving snows were common enough, and although I lived in a city we did, indeed, go to Grandmother's by sleigh, driving across town with fur rugs about our knees and bells jingling. When I used to speak of these excursions to my children, they'd look at me with a kindly tolerance. They'd never heard of such a thing—and since the city in which I spent my youth is somewhat south of the Connecticut town where I now live—they were sure I'd make it all up. But when some of our winters in this section came too soon, like an unexpected and rather unwelcome visitor—you know, the one who says "I hope I'm not too early," when, for heaven's sake, you haven't even *started* dinner—well, then my young people regarded me with more respect and decided that Mother wasn't quite demented after all.

As a child I spent many dark, autumnal days curled up in a big chair reading, with an apple within reach, if I could find one, and possibly a peppermint stick. My mother deplored this. She'd look in on me and ask why wasn't I out playing. She had a point there. But I was in, dreaming.

Nowadays, when I observe my grandchildren absorbed in books

while outdoors the sky darkens and rain starts to fall or sleet is sharp against the windowpanes, I am taken back more years than I care to count.

A warm room, preferably with a fireplace in which the flames sing their secret songs, a chair into which a small form fits as the hand into the glove, the sense of security which comes from being loved, and the adventure which meets the eye and fires the mind on every page one turns—what could be a better occupation for a November afternoon? (Provided homework and chores are done.)

Although the house in which one lives may be closed against wind, weather, and intrusion, the book one reads can open innumerable doors, to history, science, adventure, mystery, romance, and in these days, to Outer Space. But more important than this, a book serves to open the door of the individual imagination.

No wonder on this November day I think of children, known, and unknown, to me, and hope that some are curled up in chairs, like little snails in their houses, paying no attention to November weather, but reading, as once I did, and therefore lost for a little while in worlds of fantasy, magic, and high adventure.

For myself, looking back over a sometimes strange, and often disturbing, year, I find much for which to be grateful—the everyday things, the seasons; the birds flying past, or stopping off awhile to have supper or to bathe; the trees, so lavish in shade-giving this past summer; the flowers from my little garden and those brought me by friends; little trips; glimpses of great beauty; and, most of all, communication with the people I love. Perhaps this is as good a time as any to be grateful for the things I've not been granted . . . the plans which didn't mature, the dream which couldn't come true and all the things that wishful thinking shape in the mind. Perhaps if from one Thanksgiving to another I'd had all the things I hoped for, they wouldn't have been good for me.

One of the wonderful things about being a human being is that you go right on hoping. I doubt if the pattern of my hope alters much, as a great deal of it is concerned with, and for, others. I think that if you have learned never to be defeated by defeat and not to resent that a dream has vanished into limbo, and never to

8

blame anyone for the disappearance, except, perhaps yourself, you have earned the right to dream and hope again.

Now I look back, and happily, upon summer which gave me sea and sand, and lazy moon-bright nights; look back on pleasure and laughter and the idle, yet somehow important, conversations with friends and family—for even the idlest discussion is a sharing —and am grateful.

Now, most of my contemporaries are asking: Where did the summer go?

Well, into Eternity, I daresay for a little rest and a gathering up of strength for the incarnation of next year.

I find, to my distress, that I'm still difficult to live with . . . and as I live alone that means it's hard for me to live with myself. I still mislay and lose things, bark my shins, cut my fingers, and burn them, too. But this is my problem and mine alone. It's the basic weakness of not being able to conquer whatever it is that causes me to run into tables, cupboard and doors, and lose two pairs of glasses within the same hour. Now and then someone else is briefly involved, but only to the extent of helpfully trying to hunt for whatever appears to have vanished or to run for something to soothe my burn, cut, or bruise. Mainly this assistance falls upon my friends Agnes and Gussie, who have become inured to hearing me cry, "When I haven't my glasses on, how can I see to find them when they are mislaid?"

That may not make any sense, except to me and to those people who remove their glasses and then can't see where they've put them.

Sometimes I also mislay my spares.

One thing I do regret as October closes her brilliant book and November comes in and that is the loss of daylight saving. I am aware that many people do not agree with me in this, but I love the long afternoons and evenings. There's something special about a late summer day when, as shadows lengthen, the gold deepens and it's still light long after supper. And I don't in the least mind the birds waking me when it's still dark.

I admit that I look ahead with a slight shiver to ice on the roads

9

and snow, banked thick on the driveway, or blowing across it. But I've always managed to get to most places other winters or else reconciled myself to staying home. There's nothing like a really bad snowstorm to drive a person to work at a desk. So, if I've managed all these years, I'll manage in the one ahead.

Friends of mine live on a hill and below them, across the road, there's a good-sized pond where many people come to skate. If this coming winter is cold and the cold holds, the ice will thicken and hold also and young and old will flash across it in their bright winter clothes. I'll envy them as usual, for I never learned to skate. As a child, I spent a good deal of time skating flat on my face—or the reverse. I could stand up, and falter along a little if I had a chair to push ahead of me, but not if someone removed it. In Germany, during the First World War, I went to a great indoor rink where there was, even at that grim time, gaiety and color, people drinking coffee at tables above the rink, music playing, and expert instructors. As long as an instructor grasped me firmly, I could swoop and glide with the best (well, almost the best) of them. But once he took himself from my vicinity, there I was again, flat-out, on the ice.

Let's face it. I'll never learn to skate now. I'll never learn to drive a car—I'm not unhappy about that although it's inconvenient. I'll probably cook no better or worse than now; and, I'm sure, only on those occasions when I'm forced to—usually on the blizzard days. I doubt if I'll learn to sew properly, especially as needle-threading becomes more difficult even with glasses. I haven't won any earth-shaking awards—if any award is earth-shaking—nor sat at table with the Mighty and Famous. I still haven't an honorary degree, which pains me a trifle, as I yearn to be called informally, "Hey, Doc." So I'll try to be grateful for those things, too. If I learned to skate I'd probably break a leg; if I were taught to drive a car I'd undoubtedly smash it—and myself—as I'm no judge of distance. As for awards the kind I really want are not given by Kings or Committees, and I'd probably drop forks at state dinners and never, never have the right clothes to wear.

10

As for not learning to be a gourmet cook at this stage, I'm not apt to starve while I have a freezer and dare to light an oven, and the inability to sew has never distressed me, although I have trouble with slip straps and the few buttons that I firmly attach are usually crooked.

Who cares? I am often troubled by contradictory adages, aren't you? For instance, "It's never too late to learn," as opposed to "You cannot teach an old dog new tricks."

Pick your own adage. I've selected mine; the second one.

This is the time when I begin to wonder how the ornaments stacked away in the attic have fared, for it will soon be Christmas. As one grows older, psychological time speeds up. A child cannot measure the distance between one stocking-hanging evening and the next. Christmas comes, is over, and the next one seems a hundred years away. But to me it seems that only yesterday the Christmas decorations were taken up to the attic and now they must soon come down again.

Each holiday holds a deep spiritual meaning, as do the religious celebrations of all faiths, of course. And in this country the day that in many states we call Memorial or Veterans' Day, and the day upon which our country was born. On the surface each has its special tradition. I think for instance of July Fourth as a vacation-beginning time and a going-somewhere day, brilliant with fireworks. Memorial Day has meant, often, family picnics (although the weather can be cold, too). Easter is a returning to warmth and blossom; New Year's Day the opening of a new book, and Christmas and Thanksgiving are family days . . . on the surface; beneath, there is the profound meaning.

It is, I daresay, impossible to carry with us, year long, the spirit of each holiday we celebrate; the giving of Christmas, the resolutions of the New Year, the wonder of Easter, the gratitude of Thanksgiving, and all the rest. I've often wondered why Mother's Day—and Father's, too— is just one day out of the hundreds, and why people decide to love their country openly only on the Fourth of July.

11

However, I think that when the pleasure and sentiment and also the solemnity of the holidays are over for the year, we can take forward with us a little of what they mean—the inner meaning.

Giving is for any time. Not just birthdays; and goodness knows with the roster of grandchildren growing, and my many friends, I have numerous birthdays to remember.

No, I mean just giving, not of material things, but of oneself. You can't give to friend or stranger anything more welcome than attention: a valid interest in his or her problems; your own joy when they have cause for rejoicing, and understanding when there has been loss or failure.

As for Thanksgiving, one of my rare resolutions, long ago, was to thank God, every night, for the day just past, no matter what it had brought. I haven't held to it, of course; I've never, I'm afraid, kept any resolution fully, and I don't feel as guilty about it as I should because, I'm certain, very few people manage to.

Now and then, I do remember, waking, to give thanks for a night of quiet sleep, or, drifting off to that sleep, to be grateful for the good that has come to me during the day, or for any strength I have been granted to accept the less good.

Counting my blessings from last Thanksgiving to this one, I am, as my grandmother used to say, "greatly obliged" for the continuing love of my family and my friends; for the work I've been able to do, even though it hasn't been as much as I'd planned; even though, in certain instances, I've felt incompetent and frustrated. I'm obliged for unexpected gifts, most of which are intangibles, and for relaxation and fun; for heart-warming gatherings which have been mine to enjoy and remember, in this house or in the houses of others; grateful, too, for the new friends, chance-met—if we ever meet by chance those who are to become our friends—and for the swing about of the seasons: for springtime, delicate and brief; for the summer months, despite the drought; for the glorious autumn just past; and for last winter's ice and snow and their remembered beauty.

Most of all I'm grateful for all I have learned since last November. Some of it has been painful and some lessons were pricks against which I kicked violently. But here and there I have overcome a very little, and every overcoming is a victory—and so far I've been able to meet, however ineffectually, a number of everyday challenges.

Therefore on the day nationally designated as Thanksgiving in this country I shall try to remember to be grateful that I have had occasion to give thanks on more than one day in the year.

I am afraid that our national bird, the turkey, isn't grateful. But by now he must be resigned to his destiny, especially as it falls almost any day in the year and not just annually.

Pretty soon, I'll start checking the Christmas lists, adding to the one I've already made. Some things I bought last June on Long Island and last August on Cape Cod when Gladys and I had time to shop a little. These tokens are marked and put away and I hope I don't mislay them before Christmas. I've done that before. . . . As my cards were delivered in September, many of them have already been addressed. But there are always last-minute things and I try very hard not to crowd too much into those last minutes.

So now, as November ends, let's be grateful for all we have been given and for that which has been withheld, for often it is good for us not to have all that we may desire.

Let's go forward happily into winter, toward the light of the Star which shines for us all, whatever our beliefs; for a shining star is always a symbol of steadfast hope. Wherever, whenever, a star is shining and you look up and see it, there's a sort of quiet dancing in your heart.

I haven't danced, except in my heart and mind, for a great many years, but I remember the days when I did—indoors and out—the lightness, the forward-moving, and the music.

As Thanksgiving Day nears, I do not know where I'll be or with whom. I think, with close friends at their house, for the days have gone when everyone came home for Thanksgiving.

But wherever it is to be, and in whatever weather, it will be for me—and I hope for you, too—exactly what it's called: Thanksgiving Day.

13

ᴥᴥ ঃᴥ

". . . in a little crooked house."

NURSERY RHYME

In between the months, the tour . . . I often take it by myself, now I shall be companioned.

We'll start walking from the country road up the driveway which is short but, by next month, until the plough comes, it can be a weary waste of snow. At the driveway's end there's room to turn and a little red garage, a replacement for the old barn which some years ago, quietly and without complaint, fell down. And there are two red-brick paths. We'll take the one to the front door which once upon a time was a side door.

In spring, summer, and fall there's a little border along this path and beneath the small stone terrace. Now there is nothing but the bulbs and roots, invisible and waiting.

The entry hall is not very large. There's a long table and above it the portrait of my grandfather, too big for the hall, really. It belongs, by right of legacy, to my son's family; I'm just borrowing it. Sometimes, walking up the path at dusk and looking through the screen and glass of the doors, I fancy there's a man in the house.

On the table there is the old tea caddy that P. C. Wrenn sent me many years ago, with leaded compartments for tea and a sugar bowl in the middle. Beside it the Sung bowl, two pomade-jar lids, and various birds and animals in Copenhagen porcelain according to the seasons.

Nothing else except a little round table with an old lamp on it, one of my mother's straight chairs beneath an old mirror and a clothes closet. Oh, yes, between the tables there's a little hooked rug.

In this small space is contained much of my life and remembering, and to this door friends come in good or bad weather. . . .
Well, when it's very bad they take the other path to the kitchen,

14

for the stone porch entrance there is protected and this door is not. Rain pours down on the unwary.

In the thirteen years I have lived in this second edition of Fable Farm, how many people have entered the little hall—friends, acquaintances, and strangers? How many outer wrappings have been stowed away in the closet; how many storm boots flung upon its floor?

Good news has come through this door, and bad; and from the two windows on either side I can look out—onto the terrace and also into the great burning bush which stands at the left side of the steps as you enter and has to be cut back every year or you'd fight your way through it. In the autumn it is a miraculous sight, the slender leaves shading from pink to scarlet, and the birds flying in and out, seeking berries. It also offers them shelter in the winter and green, cool quiet in the heat of summer.

I must admit that I rarely use this entrance, for the keys I carry —when I don't mislay them—are for the kitchen door, which I can lock behind me without a key. But the entry hall has one practical feature: should you come in by night, you have but to reach your hand to the right to touch a switch which controls light in three places—in the pantry, at the foot of the stairs, and in the upstairs hall.

All doors lead to something . . . peace, love, and harmony or their reverse . . . some lead to the cheerful noise which surrounds a houseful of children, clattering, laughing, quarreling, singing, inquiring. Once I had a door which did just that. Some lead to quiet, as this one does.

And now before it is December, I'll take away the gourds and the porcelain birds and animals, remove the corn and the pumpkins from the outside and plan what the entry hall will offer to the visitor at Christmas time. One of the difficulties is that in order to decorate the house inside I must take so much upstairs and put it away. Sometimes I find the pomade-jar lids by Easter . . . I have an absent-minded way of storing things in unused bureau drawers for safekeeping.

No matter where I have been, or for how long, no matter how

15

pleasant a time I have had away from this "little crooked house"— not so very little as it happens—I am always glad to be back, for this is a house I trust. It is like a temporal shell about me, or perhaps it has become my personal armor. And I remember the words of Isabel Fiske Conant who said:

> "He who loves an old house
> Never loves in vain. . . ."

I love this one, despite—or perhaps because of—the plaster which cracks, the pictures which won't stay straight on the walls, the old floor boards which creak and sag a little and the vagaries of weather which bang shutters, cut off the electric power, heave shingles and create leaks.

So, from this house, we go into December.

December

Early this month the Christmas ornaments are brought downstairs and a little later the wreaths are placed on the outside doors. I like them just plain lovely green with their cones clinging to them and no artificial berries, no silvering or gilding. I also like a big red bow with no nonsense about it. And from then on I shall be continually straightening the wreaths, for the wind buffets them and it rains and snows on the red bows. I take the bows off before mid-January, but I leave the wreaths up. I like the living green which matches the tall pine and spruce trees near the house and I do not take them down until long after the holiday season.

However whipped about the wreaths, the old sleigh bells hanging where last month the multicolored corn hung, still withstand all blows, as does their worn leather strap. I rather hate to take them down and put them into the library chest, for people have fallen into the habit of ringing them when they come during the Christmas season. I often wonder where the bells came from.

It's extraordinary how tall the holly tree, given me by a dear friend a while after we moved here, has grown—bigger, fuller every year, and with a rich red increase of berries. Last year I cut some branches for the house and shall this year again before the birds have stripped it.

Thinking about house decoration I think of the families which love and adhere to tradition and also create it; most of them succeed in passing down to the next generation their special customs. I've picked up one or two myself from other people. I lived for two years in Germany during the First World War. But I didn't come home to institute the giving of gifts on Christmas Eve as my German friends always did, or the eating of carp with horseradish and cream sauce. Yet I did like the idea of each member of the family and each guest having his personal table or chair piled with gifts. When, much later, I had my own home and family, I followed this custom, too. I think it's because I'm lazy and the usual tradition of gifts beneath the tree entailed too much stooping, back-wrenching, and knocking off of ornaments. Therefore, for over forty years in this household each individual has had a sofa corner, a chair, or a table for his gifts, where he could sit—sometimes on the floor —and open them without haste. I also provide wastebaskets and scissors. So there's one German custom transplanted.

And I often think of some unknown girl, born in San Francisco or Hartford or Phoenix, who is perhaps overseas this year with her serviceman husband—Germany, Japan, anyplace—still following the familiar Christmas path of her childhood and adding something new as she goes along. A Southern woman may be reading the Christmas Carol aloud and hanging mistletoe high in a flat in Chicago or in a house in London. I spent one Christmas as a young woman in Puerto Rico; palms, not pines, surrounded us, but we gathered at one another's houses on that sugar plantation and sang the old songs and trimmed our living rooms with bright tropical flowers. There were, no doubt, Christmas ornaments to be had, but we were far from shops.

I'm sorry for those who have no traditions to remember—if it's only the placing of a shining new dime and a golden orange in a small stocking—or who, lacking them in their youth, have not created them. For this is not an outworn way of life but a continuity of gentle emotion, remembered love, and believing.

Looking back over my shoulder, a long way back, the first Christmases I recall were those after I'd turned three and we were living in an apartment in New York City. Stockings were always hung, and there was a tree, and one year during the three we lived there, a phonograph with cylindrical wax records and a great horn like a mammoth morning glory. Why I remember this so well I do not know, but it was then the final word in fashionable possessions. It's a far cry from stereo, but in those days it was just as exciting—perhaps more so—seeming a little short of miraculous.

Christmas is a time of small miracles anyway. Oh, not the suddenly transformed house, or the carols sounding everywhere; not the gifts in their bright, concealing overcoats, but the great upsurge of warmth and friendliness emanating from strangers on the streets of a city, town, or village, and from people standing together, once in a lifetime, at a shop counter. All this goes beyond the hurry, the weariness, and all the trifling annoyances which seem to beset us. Perhaps, in an earlier day, our parents and certainly our grandparents, went about their simpler planning in a more leisurely fashion; they didn't have to dive into teeming traffic; there weren't as many people to crowd into stores; and even the excitement must have been slower paced.

It usually takes me three or four hours to do the house and set worn ornaments, the crooked candles, the battered angels in their places; and to find the box which holds globes, Santa heads, and cherubs which have lost their little metal tops and can no longer be hung upon the tree. These I put into a big hurricane lamp which came to me years ago from one of my editors and his wife. It had about the rim the first mobile I'd ever seen—tiny, bright globes on wires. It also had a candle (now removed), and right on the top, a little gilt basket full of fresh garnet roses.

No roses now, just the tall lamp with a great deal of varicolored glitter inside; and the mobile still rampant.

About December twenty-first the tree things are brought down from the attic. This has happened so often in this and other houses you'd think they could spill from the cartons and boxes and climb down the attic ladder by themselves. It's an interesting

19

fancy—the birds flying, some with only one wing; the round colored globes bouncing (but not breaking); and all the tree angels marching—or winging—in pairs.

Many of my ornaments date back forty years or more, but every year some break in the process of trimming or untrimming—except of course my old Swedish wooden ones. Others just disintegrate without sound during the long months in which they are tucked away under the eaves.

When the time comes to trim, a sheet is put on the living-room couch and, with Agnes to help me and to hang some of the higher decor—the flight of angels, for instance, below the top ornament— I sort out what we have. Little by little my collection of fragile birds has diminished, but there are still a few left and there are newer ones, made of feathers or wood. For each year, and often for my birthday, friends send me ornaments. This year I'll have angels like puffs of feathers to hang, a golden cherub head given me by my daughter-in-law Peggy, two soft perfumed angels from the friends I call Royalty who live near me, and an angel all the way from Texas!

I am sure that last year there was only one Santa Claus globe left unbroken, and his beard was getting very thin. And I rather dread looking for the tiny ornament I've always called a trumpet. I rather think it's a cornet, really—all the paint's gone and last year it was showing signs of resignation to time. But I'm certain the shocking-pink carousel will be all right because it is fairly new. It came to me the Christmas of 1960, sent by my older son and his wife Janet.

I have a little trick. You know how people who skillfully wrap beautiful packages often fasten some little extra gaiety to them, usually angels mounted on pipe cleaners, or snowmen, or sprigs of artificial holly? These I save to put on the tree; and as I have had many Christmas earrings and always lose one of every pair, I save the others for hanging. And I love bells, any kind of little bells. On this tree there are also roses; one is a mink rose with a pink satin heart. It was given to me to wear long ago; the tree wears it now.

I have no great liking for "modern" decorations in the house or on the Christmas trees, however spectacular. But now that I think of it, this attitude is no longer very modern; as it's been going on for some time, perhaps another generation is following in parental footsteps. And that's fine. It's become fashionable to have a one-color tree—white, blue, pink—but I mix my colors, even those which are not supposed to be compatible, and I've never regretted it, as the over-all effect is the way a Christmas tree should look, I think—gay and shining and old-fashioned.

For various reasons, in this house I don't use tinsel or electric bulbs. I depend on lamplight or sunlight for the shining. And the days are no more when the children strung popcorn and cranberries for the enormous tree on the sun porch of the other house and also for the birds' living tree outside.

When the tree is about to be trimmed—after it's been set in its stand in the angle made by living-room bookcases—the Chinese screen and my mother's two little chairs will be moved and everything taken from the bookshelves and even the pictures from the wall. Out comes the little stepladder from the library, and a small radio in case I can find carols on it, and I try to keep one big chair uncluttered so that when my feet hurt and my back aches I can quietly collapse.

It has been years since the smell of baking permeated the house, but on Christmas Day there will be turkey roasting—and there's always the scent of pine boughs and fresh flowers. As for Christmas cookies, my neighbors, the Sisters of St. Thomas of Villanova, always bring me some from their oven, French, thin, delicate, and delicious.

Every so often I go to the big windows and watch for a special gift. The cardinals have been with me all year; in deep summer they retreated, but I could hear them speaking in the woods. This month I look for them to come to the feeder and then to trim a growing tree for me with a brief burst of scarlet. It doesn't matter whether they flash by in a gray landscape or sit like flames on a snow-covered branch, or swing down to the feeder in a winter rain.

21

Just as long as one or two come to wish me Merry Christmas, I'm happy.

All over our nation, and the world, Christmas is celebrated and also, during the early winter season, the Festival of Lights. There are few households which do not turn aside for a little while from the everyday path to rest—in spirit if not in body—to reflect and pray, each person in his own way following his own beliefs.

And everywhere little children, believing in their special miracles, are wishing for something. They won't all get what they desire, and some, perhaps, will receive far more than they should.

I wonder if my sister remembers her toy piano? I must ask her. She was very small and she longed for a toy piano at Christmas. Our parents were the most generous you can imagine, but upon that occasion my mother put down her tiny foot. "Ridiculous," she said firmly. "She'll just break it within a day."

But before Christmas came, our old cook Carrie, who rarely took a day off, put on her warm coat and bonnet and went to a department store and so my sister Esther had her piano on Christmas morning. Maybe she broke it immediately and maybe she didn't. But certainly when she looked at it under the tree, stars shone in her enormous blue eyes.

And in our Carrie's, too. If she wanted to spoil the child, well, she'd spoil her! And she spoiled me, too. I still have the heavy silver serving spoon and fork which was her wedding present to me. Wages in those days were only a fraction of wages now; but Carrie saved, and she never spent anything on herself.

This year I'll spend Christmas Eve with my old friends Mignon and Alan Eberhart as I did last year. And those of my children who are near enough to come home will do so on various other days before and after the holiday, reserving for their children, as they should, the right to be in their own homes on the Eve and the Morning. But the sleigh bells will be here for them to ring and the angels will fly all over the house, some on wings so old and fragile you'd wonder how they manage. But an elderly angel is only a matter of appearance. All angels are as young as tomorrow.

22

Toward the end of last month I had a present. A friend who had moved from this state and county five years ago and from whom I had not heard since, telephoned me. It was shortly after the assassination of the President and the darkness of that day weighed heavily upon us all. It had weighed upon her eight-year-old son, Wayne, who said that he did not want Christmas presents. He wanted, instead, to do something for someone else, and asked if he could spend his recent birthday money in that fashion.

His mother telephoned me because she knew of the school in the Kentucky mountains which I sponsor through Save the Children Federation, and she thought perhaps he could send something for the children.

So I told her what she wished to know and by now Wayne has sent his gift—and I have mine—the knowledge that there is a child who felt in a time of sorrow that he must give rather than receive.

I personally love presents, even those I cannot use; even though I long since decided not to live in a clutter and have, over the years given away things I've enjoyed over a long period of time but can no longer use. All gifts, whether you still possess them or not, are treasurable because of the love that has gone into them.

Last year, for instance, two friends made sweaters for me, and another (it is not the first she's sent me) was knitted for me by a woman who lives three thousand miles away and whom I have never met.

And upstairs in the summer closet is the gay silk dress my Peggy made for me. While on the sun porch there's a wonderful afghan Agnes made for my past birthday, and in the supply closet Gussie's apple jelly.

Despite my fretful remarks about sewing and cooking, perhaps if I had my life to live over again I'd learn—and yes, knit again, too (I did so once, during a war, and I shudder to think of the soldiers forced to wear my creations) . . . for the sheer pleasure of making things with my own hands for people I love.

What can I say about Christmas that I haven't said before and that thousands of people haven't already said? No one, not even

23

a genius, can say anything really new. We can only speak, and simply, the old truths, each in his own way; the truth of sharing, of giving, and of beauty.

Few people remain during this season in a continual state of frustration and fatigue, or reluctance. They may say, "I'm so tired I could drop!" They may seize upon their lists and look upon them with something approaching horror; they may say, "I'll be glad when it's over." But there is always that moment when the tiredness and rushing about and the general upsetment seems to vanish and all that you've done becomes beautifully worth while. For Christmas is a time of gaiety and gravity, of song and of silence, of reaching out, of expansion.

Only the truly cynical, the unloving, uncaring, and unsharing really resent this season. Or perhaps the lonely, the neglected, and the unfortunate may resent it, but in a different way, because they feel they have nothing to give. Sometimes they are granted revelation during which they realize that they still have the power to create joy. This has nothing to do with having, and spending, money but only with spending yourself, extravagantly. A lonely person can find someone as lonely, a neglected person one as neglected, and an unfortunate someone who is more forlorn.

Christmas is not all color and music, bells and candles, and gifts. It's not all tradition and memories and the delight of introducing very young people to something glittering and lovely and new to them. It is also a moment of quiet meditation, of remembering in a very personal way those who will not stand again at the door, laughing, or sit with us at the table. It is a time in which to consider another list—the list of the enduring gifts we can give to our families, to friends, and even to strangers . . . those offerings of the heart which are never purchased, being beyond price, and which are never lost or broken or put away to gather dust; the gifts of love, sincerity, and sharing; the gifts of courage and hope to those who may lack these lamps unto their feet; the gift of understanding, and the great gift of gratitude.

No matter how much or how little we may have of worldly goods, each has something to give. This is what I most want to send and to receive this year . . . a thought, a word, a card, a letter, something made by hand, something bought, not hastily but with deliberation—and always, prayer. For everyone can pray for others.

Just a little while ago I was given a gift of summer by a friend —an announcement that new rosebushes would come to me to be planted in the spring.

At this season people often send me cut flowers, which have a brief glowing life. I have a pair of porcelain angels in which a small flower arrangement came from Alma some years ago; each year I return them to her to be refilled. And when the holly is yellowed and brittle and the flowers silently lose their petals, I can think ahead to next summer's roses which were also a Christmas gift.

Christmas gives us, I think, something to take with us into the new year—a symbol of housecleaning; everything new, bright, and better. In an era of tensions, emotional disturbances, anxieties, and discouragements, few of us are totally unaffected by pressure, yet few fail to gain from the holiday a lift of the spirit and a hopeful expectancy. For Christmas somehow gives us a bridge to cross, a turn-aside for the quiet moment, filled with a music not of this earth, and with the awareness of God.

And wherever we are, in whatever state of mind, whether in pain or grief, whether we experience delight, failure, or success, we have something to give and much to receive . . . not only the things we find in our stockings or under the tree, but those which are packaged in the heart; remembrance of happiness past and hope of happiness to come; fellowship and love; acceptance of sorrow and gratitude for joy; and always the peace which passeth understanding. . . .

These are year-round gifts.

๛ ๖

"Stay, stay at home, my heart, and rest;
Home-keeping hearts are happiest."
HENRY WADSWORTH LONGFELLOW

I note that Mr. Longfellow wrote, "home-keeping," which as

far as I am concerned is somewhat different from housekeeping, whatever the dictionary may say.

From the little entry hall, from my study or from the pantry, I go into the living room. This is of so odd a shape that I cannot describe it. I've been asked to often by distant friends, "Send a sketch," they say. I can't sketch it, either; I can't sketch anything.

This room has a fireplace and a big south window—it's so hot there when the sun shines, that even in winter you can hardly sit on one of the love seats placed at right angles to it. There is also an east window and each of these picture windows has regular windows on either side; there are also casement windows. This is, in any event, a many-windowed house; and as I love light and air, it pleases me, although when the sun is bright, or the summer days hot, I close the inside shutters.

Furniture interests most people; mine is a melange of the old and new; and of battered reproductions and odds and ends . . . on one bookcase a collection of mugs which are also all over the house and frequently used for any number of purposes. On the walls, four paintings, and a woolwork picture and something I can't describe which is done in coral-colored seaweeds, very delicate.

There's also a table close to the French doors of the study on which are shells, mostly on old lacquer plates or in bowls and over this a picture created in shells, made for me by friends.

The room is all curious angles, and doesn't lend itself to big parties. I assume that, once, it was two rooms.

Not as old as Gladys Taber's matchless "Stillmeadow," which I know so well, this house was originally built around or a little prior to 1800—and of course added to and subtracted from. I was told by the previous owner that it once had Civil War porches. There are old parts and new, old floors and new, but upstairs some of the exposed beams remain. I like to try to figure out what was once what . . . but have never succeeded.

The colors in the living room are the jewel colors I best like, soft violet, faded aquamarine, and dusty pink . . . except in summer when the downstairs rooms undergo a change.

Compared to "Stillmeadow" this house, elderly though it is, is in the kindergarten, but any house which has survived several generations of wear and weather has a certain intangible feeling. I often sit in the early evening, alone, with the after-dinner cup of coffee beside me, and think about the people who have lived here before me. They breathe again in the walls and speak in the shadows. For in an old house there has been much joy and sorrow; there have been births and deaths; young people have come, early in their marriages; old people have lived out their lives.

The mulberry tree which looks into the east window and reaches above the sunroom upstairs, has been standing for uncounted years. It is enormous, although half gone from hurricanes, ice storms, and time. It bore fruit the first summer I was here and not again until seven years had passed; it has borne none since. It bestows a wonderful shade and is beloved by the birds. I pray that it lasts my time.

I've heard now and then about some of the people who once lived here; I knew only those from whom I bought the place. And thinking back some hundred and sixty-four years, I wonder what the house has silently observed. I wonder about the laughter and the weeping of its former tenants, and I wonder about their thoughts. I believe that, in the main, it's been a happy house, for there is within it a sense of quiet.

Long before I lived in an old house—the first one I owned in this state was also old, though younger than this—I wrote about old houses. I had intended to set down those lines here, but remembered that I haven't a copy of the book. I gave it to a dear friend in England some time ago. Perhaps I'll ask the friends who search for out-of-print books to see if they can find that unimportant little volume. It would be interesting to know what I felt about old houses when I was thirty.

Every house, new or old, assumes the character of the people who live in it. When the next family comes in, it retains something of those who have gone, and simply adds new atmosphere.

This is the only house in which I have ever lived where I'd be content to be alone; coming in at night, I find not just walls and warmth—or in summer, a cooling breeze—but a silent welcome, as if, despite the fact that I am lately come here—thirteen years isn't very long—I belong to the house much more than it belongs to me. For nothing material belongs to us forever.

Someday other people will live here, and I hope that I shall have left a small imprint, an invisible, intangible legacy of whatever years I was part of the farmhouse, and that they'll find happiness and serenity. For houses take the thoughts and dreams of those who love within them; they take the sorrows and the anxiety; they take the achievements and the failures and weave them into an orderly pattern of living.

So when I take people through the house, I am not really guiding, I am guided.

January

While it gives me great pleasure to wish my friends and, indeed, all the world a happy New Year, I am always a trifle astonished when the actual date appears on my calendars . . . the one which hangs in the pantry and is really a tea towel, which Gussie gives me annually, and the one on my desk, to say nothing of those which come at Christmas. . . . Even the date on my morning newspaper amazes me. Why, I don't know. There's always been a new year, on every calendar—although the dates in some instances differ—and there always will be.

I do not fancy the symbol of the New Year as a naked baby; the season here is not comfortable for little undressed children. I'd rather the year was symbolized as someone strong, mature, and ready to meet any challenge, someone with the past behind him from which he has learned, and the future ahead. For there will be many challenges to meet in our personal lives, in the life of our community and nation. These occur every year.

Always, a year is ushered in with noise and excitement; there will be parties, special television programs, dancing and music; and hordes of people will crowd into Times Square in New York City. In fact, in every city there will be a seething mass of people gathered together. Bells will ring, whistles blow, and in the churches there will be prayer; and prayer in the hearts of a great many of us also, as a year slips into eternity and another is born into sidereal time.

In this uncertain climate the year can come on white and silent feet; it can dawn in smoky-gold or rush in on the wings of a blizzard or an ice storm. However, it comes and in whatever way we greet it, it will remain with us for twelve months and no more.

Actually, I'm cheating a little for, as I write, we're halfway through the month. This little book, which is based on material prepared months ago as well as on new material, I began to put together one Sunday evening; I got as far as a title, a foreword and a dedication, and the following day awakened to a wild screaming wind and tons of snow. So I went seriously to work. For there's nothing like being marooned, as it were, to make work a pleasure.

As a matter of fact, last year we had snows before Christmas, and exceptionally nasty ice, sleet, freezing rain, and snow on New Year's Day which, as I went out with friends, I know made for precarious driving. New Year's Eve had been fine and very cold.

The house, right after January first, was restored to its workaday appearance. I still have two mugs of holly in the study; and on the living-room desk the little angels continue to bear frosted sprigs of green; on the hearth there is a big floor vase of pine branches holding their scent, and with them forsythia which I cut during a warmish spell before Christmas, and have been thinking of discarding because they have just been sitting there, doing nothing. But Agnes told me today that they have made up their minds to bloom. If so it will be lovely. Snow outside and—today—sunlight and indoors a shower of sun in forced forsythia bloom.

I have a cowardly attitude toward winter. I'm scared of too much ice and snow. And I don't make resolutions; I know myself too well. But this is a time when most of us try to balance the accounts, and I don't mean merely checkbooks, ledgers, and budgets. We look back, in a quiet hour, and endeavor to review the year just gone, asking ourselves: What have I accomplished?

30

Where have I failed? What has been written down in black ink and how much is set forth in red?

It's a time for backward looking, I think, for only when we look back with clear eyes can we learn to see ahead. For all we did or didn't do last year can fashion the mold for this one. I do not mean that we should live in last year's figurative house or go prowling through it, opening doors upon sorrow, mistakes, and fleeting joy. I mean, simply to look back in a spirit of realistic inquiry which is to evaluate. I can honestly say that, in the year which has vanished, I did many things I wish I hadn't; said much I wish I could recall and, more important, even thought things I wish I had not: unkind, negative, destructive. For all thought, however trivial-seeming, however fleeting, is immeasurably powerful.

Every season has its imperfections and also its consolations. In winter, for instance, there are no insects, no humidity; there are glowing fireplace fires and snowed-in days when you can't go anywhere, so you stay home and find time not only to work but to read and to ponder, or just to be lazy, which is something of a lost art. It is not a question of usefully employing leisure time—often when you have it, you wear yourself out finding things to do, or wondering *what* to do. I mean just doing absolutely nothing for half an hour or even ten minutes.

Last summer, when I was with my sister, we went down to a part of the beach which affords an unusual view—the ocean, a short walk across the sand, and on the other side of the sand a fresh-water pond. Near that, sheltered by a dune, we saw a little boy lying flat on his stomach with his face on his arm. He wasn't doing anything. He wasn't playing, or stirring, and his family—another older boy, a young woman, and a dog—were some distance away. And the little lad himself was singing quietly and tunelessly.

He wasn't building sand castles, he wasn't talking to anyone. He was just lying there in the sun, singing to himself and, I am certain, dreaming. This is wonderful because in our extremely organized society there seems to be so little time in which to permit a child—let alone adults—to be idle, to think and to dream.

So I think I'll take time out. This isn't a resolution, of course; it's just a hope. I'll try, anyway, during this year to indulge myself occasionally in lovely nothingness, not even reading or doing crossword puzzles, not looking at television or writing the letters I've put off answering.

Perhaps I'll even attempt to conquer the furniture which trips me maliciously when I'm not looking, and my attraction to open doors, including those of supply closets. I run into them more often than you'll meet a friend downtown.

I'll try to work when I should and play when I can, but in between take a little breather in which to "loafe and invite my soul," as Walt Whitman said. I hope the invitation is accepted.

During the recent storm, after the wind had died down for a while, I thought, as I always do, that there's nothing as silent as snow falling when it's not driven against the panes. And silence is salutary.

Much of life consists of sounds, especially the sound of words—everywhere, in houses, on streets, in buses, planes, trains, motorcars. We are spoken to from lecterns, from radios, from motion-picture and television screens. Many of us love words for their own sakes, for their sounds and meanings. I do and always have, and I have some special favorites. Most of us, however, do not take full advantage of even the average vocabulary, but use what comes to hand, or rather, tongue. Some time ago—I think, in 1952—I watched a motion picture being made, which was later shown on television. There was no dialogue at all; there didn't have to be. It ran for a full hour, without a word being uttered. There was background music and also the normal noises which are all about us; the sound of footsteps, running or walking; the opening of desk and bureau drawers and of a safe; the sound of a key turning in a lock.

There were people talking in the streets or on stairways, but the words were muffled, not discernible to the ear. Doors opened and closed; papers crackled; a file was slid out and then slammed back. There were the sounds of radios and recorders playing; once or twice someone sighed, and later you heard a high wind blowing across the top of a tall building. There was the sound of a coffee cup being placed upon a saucer and that of a telephone ringing and of coins tinkling into the phone-booth slots. There was the sound created by the opening of a suitcase; there was children's laughter and the vibrating roar of buses and automobiles. Each of these sounds became more definite and meaningful than usual, for there were no words to accompany them.

I thought of how much, how constantly, we use words and how often wrongly; and that in very important moments we sometimes use none at all; for instance, in the wonder of marvelous delight, during the shock of sudden sorrow, or in times of intense fear.

There are many speechless occasions when no words are necessary; perhaps the right ones haven't been invented.

The silence of the first big January snow can be merciful, once the wind ceases, even if roads are blocked and men are working overtime out in the bitter cold. In silence the snow covers the bare ground and bough, ugly places and sleeping roots of grass and flowers. It falls through the night as we sleep, and often after we have awakened. But we know that, if not today, then tomorrow or the day after the sun will emerge, the sky will be blue, and the world a white brilliance all around us, still wrapped in the blanket of silence.

During the storm I went out to the bird feeders, and the next day someone went for me and brushed the snow from the shelves and put in more seed. The birds, beaten by the winds, had had a rough time. When the wind ceased and the sun came out, they were back at the feeders, thinking, I daresay, that they'd waited too long to go South. Some, however, belong here, year round; and perhaps they thought of spring.

One unimportant thing I noticed only last night, when I switched on the light over the back porch and went to empty my wastebaskets into the huge one which stands there. Its contents, the debris of several days of living, were covered with snow, so you didn't see anything torn up, or discarded; just snow.

You may have noticed that I didn't wish for anything last month except for my feathered cardinals' dazzling blessing. But I do wish for certain qualities during this new year, and these gifts no one can give me; I must renew or discover or create them within myself.

Patience, for instance; strength and humility. These are the most desired, and after these the ability to go on working—and better than I have worked in the past—and the difficult quality of being able to take things a step at a time.

Trust, I have always had, and faith. But trust is like a candle; it burns brightly at times, at others it wavers, and sometimes it goes out, leaving darkness for a while, until we find a star by which to relight it. Faith is not a candle; it is a glow, sometimes dim, sometimes radiant.

Man's little world, though sometimes filled with fear and distrust, has great natural beauty which man often destroys, in ignorance or greed, but sometimes in order to achieve. But from that sort of destruction often a stark sort of beauty arises—the factory, the laboratory.

And man's world has become a nervous one, encompassed by anxiety. God's world is other than this; always balanced, calm, and in order.

Someone wrote me a while back, "I am telling you this because I think you understand me."

Well, perhaps I did, perhaps I did not; it is one thing to understand with the mind; to that you must add also the heart. It is not easy to understand anyone wholly, even those closest to you; and no one, however helped by science, fully understands himself.

Perfect comprehension belongs to God's world, and not to ours. The most we can do is try.

All of us criticize others; make hasty, ill-considered judgments; and forget to look upon both sides of the coin. And if you're like me, there'll be times when you do not make an effort to understand something which is perhaps alien to you, your way of life, or thought.

So I think I'll ask for yet another New Year's gift, that of understanding, however small the package in which it comes—the package being myself.

I suppose the best New Year's present we can give ourselves, our families, friends, and neighbors is to try and bring into man's world, through our own thinking, trust, and faith, a little of God's world and its infinite beauty.

Everyone can create for himself something of this other atmosphere, through his thought, his sharing, and his loving. I contemplate the many people I know who meet their everyday problems, who give of themselves and who love—both personally and impersonally—and it is as if each of these moves in his own particular illumination, a small circle of golden light, which you, looking at him, cannot see but can feel.

I am most grateful for—and to—those of my friends who by a word or two or just by silence and example, have shown me this light. Looking ahead as, of course, we must, I desire in the year just beginning, to catch and keep some of that radiance myself.

Nothing in man's world is perfect and all is subject to attack—the roses in your garden, the trees in your yard, the security of your thinking. Wonderful machines are built, labor-saving devices, cars to devour the miles, airplanes to minimize distance, computers which practically think; yet all these are also subject to stresses and to failure.

So are we, as each year—sometimes forewarned, but more often not—we face attack from illness, from grief, from despair and from the pain we feel for others. But only by meeting the attack can we grow and learn and acquire a little, the wisdom of understanding.

Many of our failures are, I think, based upon the inability to understand both our own situations and the situations of others. In the latter case, it is hard to walk, even briefly, in the shoes of another person, or upon his personal path. It is easy to pass judgment upon his mistakes or dismiss his difficulties as having been self-incurred. But understanding him, even in the smallest degree, changes the viewpoint drastically; it's as if you came out of darkness, or twilight, into the morning.

What this new year will bring me I do not know. I like to think that I'll be able to accept in silence whatever it may bring of difficulty, or that, confronted with someone else's trouble, I can find the few, right words. For, as it has been said, there is a time to keep silent and a time to speak.

It has also been said that we bring nothing into this world and take nothing with us when we depart. But that was written of material possessions. All of us bring with us the need to love and to be loved and take with us, in spirit, the knowledge of having loved and having been loved. As the infant grows and the formative years begin, this necessity for giving and receiving is conditioned by many things: environment, circumstances, the people around us, the discovery of personal prejudice, the emotional drives, and the opinions toward which they lead us. Often we find ourselves able to receive, yet not to give; or able to give, but feeling we have had little in return. Yet the basic needs remain. You see them in the baby barely conscious of the world about him, recognizing only sound, light and darkness, hunger and a groping for security; you see them in a frightened child who feels that he hasn't a friend, and, perhaps, has not; and in the old man dreaming in the sun, alone, unless, perchance, he has his dog beside him, in which case he can both give and receive.

So in the new year I wish for hours of work, for the lazy interludes, and companioned relaxation; I wish for silence and for speech and always for the capacity to love and to be loved. I wish for the ability to remember the good things and forget the rest, to create new memories and to be sustained by trust and hope and courage; and always to try to understand.

What else is really important in any year?

"O Winter, ruler of the inverted year! . . .
I love thee, all unlovely as thou seem'st,
And dreaded as thou art. . . .
I crown thee king of intimate delights,
Fireside enjoyments, home-born happiness."

WILLIAM COWPER

I do not know that I wholly agree with Mr. Cowper. My love for winter is somewhat more temperate than the season itself, but I do admit the intimate delights and the fireside enjoyments.

Today, facing February, the sun shines valiantly, but makes very little progress as far as melting the snowbanks is concerned. I arrived at my desk in a terrible temper, having cast a glass of cranberry juice in all directions, stabbed myself with scissors and, while scrubbing the bathtub, seen the sponge I was using quietly disintegrate.

So I think I'll go into the kitchen, pour another beaker of cranberry juice—which, of course, always reminds me of Cape Cod—and, grasping it firmly with both hands, take a look around.

I have been told that once this house had no kitchen. This I do not believe; people must have had some place in which to cook; they don't just live on air. Perhaps a little ell, now vanished? When we came here to live, there was a small salt box down the slope, near a stone wall. It had once been part of the house, I was informed. Summer, kitchen, or woodshed? I'll never know. A previous owner had more or less fixed it up as a playhouse for her grandchildren. I intended to restore it to something resembling a studio for my daughter Ann. But she went to a Western state before we moved and returns here only for rare visits. So the salt box is silently crumbling away; vines cover it, bushes grow thick about it, and nuts drop upon the battered shingles from a tree above. And our last little dog, Taffy, is buried beside it.

The kitchen is cold. I don't know why, exactly, but for the past

37

two seasons we've managed to keep it moderately comfortable. It is also big, and, Gladys Taber says, impractical. But that's the way it's going to be for my time. I've not done anything for it but paint a new floor (less lethal than the original cement) and add a couple of new counters.

There's a pantry, as you look toward the dining room; and this still has the old floors, as has the dining room itself. The dining room is small. I can—but seldom do—seat and serve eight; I could seat more if I put another leaf in my mother's oval table—but then no one could move around it. The ceiling at one end is cracking again; it hasn't been redone since 1956, and I note with some embarrassment that if it falls during some dinner hour, it will crash upon guests and not the mistress. Perhaps, if I go away in March, it can be remedied then, but I do not want to be here with all that dust and uproar and the moving out of table, server, and chairs; the old corner cupboard is full of Chinese porcelains and these, too, will have to be moved. What I do not see (or hear) won't worry me, I hope.

A dining table, close relative of the kitchen stove, is the home's center. The shape—square, round, oval—doesn't matter. Nor does it matter whether it is in the kitchen or a corner of the living room. It doesn't even matter if it isn't a table at all, but simply a lot of trays on legs.

The important thing is who sits with you . . . family, old friends or new; and that the gentle art of conversation be practiced. Time out to talk and discuss, not simply state opinions, or say "Please pass the salt."

My older daughter, her husband, and their six children, who range in ages from nineteen to eight, have an enormous table in the kitchen (I don't think they ever use the dining room). They can seat nine people (I know, as I've often had supper and lunch there) and probably more. It saves steps. At breakfast time not everyone is there at once; all the children appear to have different times for attending school. At lunch, the rule is: Make your own sandwich, pour your own milk, put the coffee on for the adults. But dinner is a very lively affair.

38

Many of my meals are taken alone. Several days a week I am indulged at breakfast with a bedside tray. (That's why the cranberry juice spilled over the blanket cover, the electric blanket, and a sheet this morning.) On the days when I fend for myself, I set up my tray on a small kitchen table. Home, most days, for lunch I have a tray by the south window in the living room. Nights, I eat sedately in the dining room and do not read as I do other times: newspapers at breakfast, a book or magazine during lunch. After-dinner coffee accompanies me back to the love seat beside the pink coffee table in the living room.

I try not to hurry too much over solitary meals, but I do not always succeed in establishing leisure. Which reminds me that I'm still endeavoring to find the do-nothing moments. I haven't been at this project too long and now and then I do manage, but a restless mind is something I must first subdue. Sitting idly, I find myself thinking of all that has to be done, with muscles tensed to leap up and do it. But here and there I have won a victory. Usually I take this type of siesta in the sunroom, having banished books, cross-word puzzles, and pencils. It is easiest at sunset. I have never seen as consistently lovely winter sunsets as of late. They began in October really and they are like flowing gold, crushed rose petals, all the colors of the autumn trees melted together; and, of course, in winter there are usually pools of that clear pale green which seem particularly to belong to winter. . . .

This time I drank the cranberry juice without disaster, so I'll leave the kitchen and return to the study. From my desk I can see part of the dining room, the miniature hall, and, if I lean to the left, part of the enclosed stairs.

Although I am alone as I begin my day's work here, I know that no one is ever truly alone. Each of us—though upon occasion not physically companioned—is surrounded by so much: the world outside, the little world of home, the memories of those who have been with us, the anticipation of those who will come again; the thoughts of those who love us and pause in whatever they are doing to think of us.

February

This is the month of hearts and hothouse flowers, of Abraham Lincoln and George Washington; to say nothing of the many people I know who have birthdays during February. One, now in Germany, smack dab on Valentine's Day.

This is a month which may come in on a burst of sunlight, in a spatter of rain, sometimes freezing, or with a great onrushing of snow. There'll be ice on the brick walls and on the steps too; and if I don't slip there, I'm apt to skid on the waxed and polished floor when I come inside and remove my stadium boots.

I've bought lots of valentines, and have already addressed a few. I just hope I don't forget to mail them. Frequently, feeling rather smug, I address birthday cards weeks ahead, and squirrel them away. Then the right date comes and goes and a month later I find the cards.

Finding things reminds me of a white sale I attended last month in a nearby town. First I found that the charge-plate I had with me was not the correct one; then I mislaid it and when I went on to another department, I discovered that I didn't have even the wrong plate. I trekked back to the linen counter and spoke to the attractive girl who had helped me there. She suggested that I turn out my handbag. I did—and there was the plate.

Later, when I reached home, my door key was missing. I let myself in anyway, for I learned long ago to secrete a key outside where only the birds and I can find it.

Then I wrote to the pretty girl in "Linens," whose name I had taken pains to learn. I explained my absent-minded-professor nature, enclosed a stamped addressed envelope and waited, trusting that I'd dumped the key out with the rest of the clutter in the handbag. I had. The key came back.

Now perhaps I should write myself a note and say: Remember to mail valentines.

Originally these were designed to be sent anonymously by the hopeful—and also the hopeless—lover, but times have changed. Now we sign our sentimental missives as a rule, and there are cards designed to send to anyone and everyone—friends, teachers, great grandmothers—you name it, you can buy it.

Now and then one comes to me which contains elements of astonishment. These arrive any time of the year, not merely in February. Some time ago, for instance, a stranger sent me a photograph of my husband taken before I knew him and one I'd never seen. It had belonged to her mother who'd been, I think, a distant relative of his family.

Another time—and from another stranger—a flat gold pencil came, which had been designed to wear on a watch chain. She said it had been in her family for forty years and she thought that it had once belonged to my father.

The pencil is in a gold case, set with three red stones and I doubt that the flat leads which would fit into it are made any more. On the back of the case is my father's full name.

I'm not certain that I remember the pencil. Still, he must have worn or carried it for sometime. There's a dent here and there, as if some enterprising child had thoughtfully chewed upon it. Myself, my sister, or someone in that other family? I've given it to my younger son who was named for my father and he can keep it for his son who also bears the same name.

For a time I carried the pencil in a button-down section of my billfold and I'd take it out now and then and hold it in my hand and think of my father and of the many times he must have held and used it.

This is a little link—as is the photograph—between me and the past; and both gifts were given me by women I'd never met but who, through their generosity, sent me thoughtful valentines, no matter what the calendar read.

I've had other such gifts, too: one an old photograph of my paternal grandfather as a young man; another a daguerreotype, which the sender thought was of my grandfather and his first wife. I honestly don't know. But I have kept them, with pleasure.

Valentines, signed or unsigned, can reach us at any season. And the February fourteenth symbol of a heart, transfixed by an arrow, is an excellent one, for hearts are always being transfixed by love, by hope, by amazement, and thankfulness.

Valentines should not be thrown perfunctorily into a letter box but dropped with the gentle touch of friendship and affection, with the desire to reach out to someone with the golden arrow of our thought. I think we should open those we receive, not only with pleasure or amusement—for some of the modern cards are very amusing—but with gratitude. Too often we say, "How nice," or something equally tepid, and toss the cards aside, except perhaps, for a special few.

Cards handmade by children are, I think, particularly dear. Much effort and time, much wracking of little minds and cramping of small fingers have gone into the sometimes startling creation of a lopsided heart, of an arrow off its mark, or of curious trees and stranger flowers, which have grown nowhere save on these bits of paper. Usually there's printing beneath the picture and usually, too, it says "with love."

Anything given in love should so be received. There are as many kinds of love, I daresay, as there are valentines, but each springs from the same source and each is valuable.

I know of no better way to spend a long February evening than in looking over the cards I've shopped for and attempting to address the right one to everyone on the list. I remember when I was young that on the backs of envelopes (or under the stamp) someone, greatly daring, would print S.W.A.K.—sealed with a kiss. All valentines should be so sealed, in thought, if without the code.

I doubt if many young people nowadays condescend to such sentimentality. If they do, they express it differently. The ways of youngsters, when I was one, were rather timid, absurd, and charming, but tentative temerity doesn't seem to be compatible with the era of the fast car and even more lethal diversions. It seems to me that despite the forward thrust of so-called progress, it would be pleasant to preserve some of the old-fashioned ways.

When the heart speaks, it should be heard, no matter how young—or old—it is. Once hearts remained young for quite a while. Now, with little girls wishing to go "formal," to say nothing of "steady" at eleven, and crying out for the not-so-distant moon of high heels, lipstick, and floor-length frocks, it's something else again. Or is it? Perhaps the heart which yearns to beat beneath a low-cut bodice is still young.

At this point I am happy to remark that the girl grandchildren I have who have reached the ages of something over eleven and something over thirteen have not been permitted this leap into pseudo maturity, even though they may say they have the meanest parents on the block!

Youth is not forever, except in the spirit, and I feel a trifle melancholy when I see grown-up—well, slightly grown-up—infants denying youth. For it does not come again and if they are swept into the stream of progress this early, what's left at, say, eighteen?

That which separates one generation from the next has been explained, I daresay, through all generations . . . the world changes, becomes smaller; life grows more precarious; manners, modes, and mores alter, and what was once tabu is now permitted.

The gulf of a generation separated me from my parents (as I am now separated from my children), but I remember quite well that

I was on many occasions, willful, restless, contrary, and probably very hard to endure.

Still there was a check; several checks in fact. Respect, as I recall it, for one's elders—no matter how much one grumbled about them privately—and for authority, which in many families nowadays does not seem to exist. My parents made certain demands, backed them up, and enforced at least outward obedience no matter how much I muttered in my rebellious mind.

In those days young men came calling. Who hears of such a thing nowadays? Now they sit outside in Dad's sports car, or even in their own, and lean heavily upon the horn. But in the years when young men called formally upon young women there was a going-home time. At eleven, my father either dropped—or flung—his shoes, quite noticeably in a room above the parlor or else came romping downstairs to remark, "How nice to have seen you . . . good night . . . I hope you'll come again?"

All very dull and passé, of course, but serving a purpose.

A friend of mine, who is close to me, once remarked that in a sense parents are like a door that can be closed against danger to their children; one that can be shut with the children inside, not as in a prison cell but as within a warm, safe shelter; and also a door that can open wide on vistas of knowledge, understanding, and spiritual instruction.

We can debate for hours about what keeps the generations apart. What holds them together is simple: it is love, sharing, respect—each for the other—and comprehension.

When the teenagers give a party and the parents go out that's indulgence. "Leave the kids to themselves," they say, "they don't want us around." And perhaps the parents don't want to be around. But sometimes such gala occasions end in complete disaster and then the parents ask, in shocked bewilderment, "What did we do?" It isn't so much what they did, it's what they didn't do, not just upon that particular evening but during all the years before it.

If you had a little child you wouldn't turn it loose on the city streets without explaining the meaning of the red and green and yellow lights. This is discipline, it is teaching, it is also a warning and, for the child, a sense of security. In my experience, children like discipline, no matter how much they may contend that they hate it. It is a solid structure of security, it symbolizes the fact that their parents love them, that they care what their children do, and what they become.

Every generation gives its children to the world, and into the keeping of those children, once grown, the world itself. If we have not kept them safe, what will happen to the world they must inherit?

Some time ago I had a letter from a teenage girl. She said, among other things, "My parents let me do anything I want to. I wonder, sometimes, if they care about me, at all?"

We know that when the shortest day, which is in December, has come and gone, the days begin to lengthen, however imperceptibly, but it isn't until about mid-February (at which time in this section we are apt to have horrendous storms) that we turn our faces toward the spring, and that's a valentine, however much the snow dances about us; a gift of love from nature and the Creator of all things; the warming sun; the stirring of earth in her frozen sleep; the promise of the first migratory bird; the first pale, fragile snowdrop; the first faint intimation of glory to come.

Signed or unsigned, a valentine.

Here, where I live, February can be a stern and unrelenting month, and this year it has an extra day as it's Leap Year. Many people have been born on February twenty-ninth and take pleasure, publicly (if not privately) in having a birthday only once in four years. But whether it has twenty-eight or twenty-nine days the month is short, and always a forerunner of spring, no matter how severe the weather, how deep the snow and penetrating the frost, nor how much below or above zero the thermometer reads. Last winter was a real dilly, or as *Hazel* of cartoon and television fame would say, a doozie (I sometimes wonder which is my closer friend—Hazel; her prototype on the screen whom I have never met; or Ted Key, her creator, whom I know very well.)

This winter started out both dilly and doozie. I don't know how or when it will end, but I do know that this month, as every month, I look back to time elapsed; the happiness, the warmth of the Christmas season; the promise of the New Year, even though it arrived in snow flurries, ice, and with inconvenience, even danger, in its chilly hands. Also I look ahead to spring and to the summer which must inevitably follow. This is important; if we look back, we must also look ahead; and we must also, by all means, face the present moment squarely; for except in memory and in hope, all we really possess is the Now.

Perhaps next month, if all goes well, I'll be able to return to Florida where I'll visit my lifetime friend, to whom this book is dedicated, and later go to be near a daughter-in-law, whose name is also Janet . . . but at this writing I do not know. I am still trying to take things a step at a time and to "play it by ear," despite the distressing fact that I am probably tone deaf. This is unfortunate, as in church, for instance, I sing in a sort of curious tuneless basso profundo though the melody inside my head is clear and on key.

To look back, to look ahead, and at the same time to be able to live in the immediate present—this is a magic quality which we have all been given. We know that the past has gone, leaving its residue of good or evil; we know that the moment in which we must live is Now; and we know equally that the future is veiled. Tomorrow is, in a very real sense, never. We wake and say "it's tomorrow," but by that time it's really today and today is all we may rightfully claim.

Each year, month, week, day, hour is as an unopened package until it arrives. We do not know what it will hold, but if we have grown a fraction wise, and have stayed spiritually young, while growing a little older we can face what is to come with hope and at least a semblance of fortitude.

"Fortitude"—that's one of my favorite words, along with "dusk" and "light" and "starry."

46

Last year, at this time, I had many valentines from people I know, from people I've never met and also one from a friend I'd not seen or heard from in a quarter of a century. She wrote on the card that while she was shopping she suddenly thought of me. The card had gone first to an address at which I haven't lived for years, but it did reach me, as the arrow its mark, after a slight deviation in course.

Such a remembering seems to me a minor miracle and I wondered then, as I still do what made her think of me as she walked through a shop, pausing at a counter to look over the many bright cards, and reach for the one she sent to me.

I've a friend in England from whom I rarely hear, as his wife does the social writing, but every valentines season for some years past he's managed to find for me a charming card, having, as his wife once wrote, combed through every shop in London. Last year's card, however, he bought in Belgium and its printed message was couched in French—so I had to draw upon my dim remembrance of schooldays and the classroom to translate it. I didn't, however, have to translate the fact that he thought of me and addressed the special card in his own quite beautiful handwriting.

Sometimes, in a manner of speaking, we have to translate our own language—one with which we have been familiar from infancy—in order to arrive at a correct interpretation of someone else's thought.

If, in March, I fly away on the wings of some kindly airline, the weather may well be stormy. Since I like to be at the airport an hour ahead of flight time I have in the last few years gone to the airfield the night before, and stayed at the hotel there, rather than expose myself to the pressure of racing to catch a plane toward which I must be driven over difficult roads. Last year, it didn't start to snow until I was crossing that field, and I arrived in Tampa under a hot and blazing sun. . . . I must admit that even last month I was already weary of pulling storm boots on and off; of struggling through drifts to feed the birds; of getting in and out of sweaters, ancient but protective fur coats, or heavy tweeds.

47

But it won't last forever; it never does; and probably six months from now, when I hope I'll be at the Cape, if it dares to be too hot or even a little humid, I'll be complaining about that, too.

The human memory is long and tenacious where pain, grief, humiliation, disappointment, or upsetment, are concerned. It is shorter, I fear, when it looks back upon blessings; and shorter still when it considers past weather.

I've always been alarmed at the thought that one day I might have to stand in a witness box and be asked: What were you doing on June 21, 1948? I wouldn't know, unless that had happened to be my wedding day (which it wasn't) or the day on which I had a baby or won the Nobel prize. Or, maybe had fallen downstairs.

It would be even worse to be asked under oath: "What was the weather like eight months ago today?"

This year with Easter coming early, Ash Wednesday arrives on Mr. Lincoln's birthday. On that day I'll be speaking at a church luncheon so now I'm asking myself: What shall I advise my audience (and myself) to give up for Lent?

I think I know.

Abstinence and sacrifice at certain seasons is not confined to the Christian religion; those of the Jewish Faith, of the Hindu and of Islam, also have their times of fasting and relinquishing.

Sometimes people abstain for forty days from things they should have given up long since, perhaps for always, because, for instance, of their health. Material abstinence even for forty days does exercise the spiritual muscles, for it is self-discipline. But there are other abstinences. I am sure there are things we could all give up, and for all time, provided we have the strength: the sweetness of revenge; the bitter herbs of resentment; the sharp spices of gossip; the bland puddings of complacency; the ego-building proteins of vanity; the strong stimulant of prejudice, whether religious, racial, or intellectual; the heavy bread which nourishes unkindness, and the drugging wine of self-pity.

These are spiritual daily fasts and they take more will power than most of us have to begin and to stay with them.

48

"Here stand my books . . ."

ANDREW LANG

In this room, which I do not call a study (I do very little studying here) but a workroom, I spend a large part of my time. At the typewriter I face the fireplace and its mantel laden with white mugs, the representations of Buddha and Kwan-Yin, the Madonna painted for me on a wood panel by a friend. There are pictures facing me also. And if I turn my chair to the big desk, I face a wall of books and, after two windows have interrupted, another bookcase and a smaller one to my right. So as Mr. Lang said, "Here stand my books." Those on the desk itself are dictionaries and the like.

Though I've never had a workroom as pleasant as this (it has three windows looking south and two west), I've worked in many rooms; in hotel bedrooms, some perishing cold, in other climates; in a quiet little house on Cape Cod; in a sun porch, turned workshop, in my first Connecticut house; and in a quite big library in Brooklyn, New York. Actually the first country house had a library too, quite imposing, but I didn't work in that one. There were so many books there that I had to dispose of numbers of them when I moved here; and I'm still doing it.

I've never worked, really, on a plane, but often in train compartments. And I daresay I could, if necessary, work in a boiler factory because I became conditioned very early to household and outside noises and to what is sometimes called the patter of little feet. Actually, little feet don't patter for long; they grow bigger and stomp.

I am also conditioned to interruptions. Phones ring . . . I answer. The doorbell chimes . . . I run to the side door and peer out, or to the kitchen, as I never know which one is ringing. I am accustomed also to people coming and going, asking questions or merely stopping by to visit.

49

I know a good many writers who refuse interruptions. One of my good friends won't answer his telephone except when his wife calls from her New York office. I haven't figured out what kind of a special signal she uses. Otherwise their youngest son does the answering when he gets home from school.

I know writers who work behind closed doors, to which people tiptoe, bearing trays, which must be very nice. I also know some who have workrooms or offices or whatever you want to call them outside of their homes and go to them regularly as any man or woman to business.

This is fine I suppose for disciplining one's creative urge, but I couldn't get used to it; I'd be lonely, or feel left out.

Work—no matter what you do—is, aside from the necessity of doing it, a panacea, perhaps even a form of escape. When you're working—writing, painting, acting—you can't think about yourself; you are forced to set aside, for the duration, your personal problems.

Today I am alone, as I usually am, particularly after the noon hour. It is a day when Agnes does not come and, as it happens, Gussie won't either because I'm going out to dinner. No one has been here except the milkman and a friend who stopped by to pick up the outgoing mail. Around twelve I went outdoors into the brisk cold air, with snow under my feet, to get the incoming mail and to feed the birds. It is one of the days on which I fight work. I answered the mail; I glanced through two magazines; I found myself a cold chicken leg and a glass of milk and took my time about consuming them. I washed the plate and the glass and then, embued by the spirit of orderliness, wiped fingerprints from cupboards and refrigerator.

But there always comes a time when—unless you are flat in bed with the flu or something—you can no longer put off doing what you must do and what, really, you want to do, though not just this minute.

I keep thinking ahead to March and wondering what that madcap month will bring me. The sun's been bright for several days and hot, but the air is very cold; the snow melts only on the roads.

And shortly after my chicken-leg break the clouds began to slip across the sky; now there's more charcoal in them, and more gray over all than blue. So perhaps it will snow again, though we haven't had much of a breather since the last time.

Under the fireplace mantel there is now an American eagle made of metal and painted in dull gilt after an old pattern. My son-in-law made it for me for Christmas. There is also a small horseshoe, with the ends properly up so the luck doesn't run out. I got that some years ago, when visiting a reproduction village in which there was an authentic blacksmith in a reproduction old blacksmith shop. To amuse the customers he hammered out these little horseshoes. Hanging near it on the fireplace, there's an ornamented Chinese container made of wood. I forget what it was for . . . Matches, perhaps? The room—in fact, the whole house—is full of Chinese things, and some East Indian, to which I recently added an Amerind wooden object which my older grandson brought me from the Adirondacks; whether or not it's authentic I can't say and don't care.

The ivories and the porcelain pieces, mostly old, and from a number of countries, are scattered around from dining room to living room to bedroom.

So I've a sense of living with several cultures and with a great many craftsmen, most of whom have long since gone from their particular senses. And some of the idle time I've talked of I can spend wondering about them, the period and circumstances in which they lived and practiced their arts.

I look, too, at the bookshelves and think about the people who wrote the books—some are still writing, but others, not—and the volumes are a complete melange on all sorts of topics and from various eras. Once, on a tour, I went through a house built about 1900 and kept as a show place and, by trying to read book titles—and succeeding to some extent—I found out what the woman who'd built the house had been interested in. You'd never find out here. My books—though they stand side by side in seeming affability or neighborliness and do not even jostle one another or object when some have to be inserted sideways—would never give

51

a clue to my preferences, for, in content, they are wildly incompatible. You'll find on these shelves fiction, nonfiction, research material and reference books which, if they had their choice, wouldn't, as we say, be found dead next to one another.

I even have some of the novels I adored when young—very bad novels I'm sure now, but I've kept them for what they meant to me then—and of course a few childhood books which will always be immortal, such as *Alice* and *The Wind in the Willows*. The rest my children have.

It would be difficult for me to live without books and I am grateful both for those I have been able to keep and for others I have known, though now discarded or given away. I am grateful also for this quiet workroom and for the trees outside, big trees with huge trunks, and for the sun that now slants through the west window, for it's after three o'clock.

Very precious and necessary to everyone is a place, no matter how small, which is quiet and in which he can work or think and dream, and a window—a material window, or a spiritual one—through which the rising or setting sun can reach him.

March

If you are unwise, or a gambler at heart, you may open your door to March and what will you find on the doorstep? A veil of rain, a flurry of snow, a glaze of ice . . . or a sweet young spring wind? Lion or lamb, which is it?

Last year, when I was going south I arranged to stay at the airport the night before my scheduled flight. I arrived in time to check in and have dinner with a friend, and the next day I had breakfast in my room, sauntered to the field, had some coffee there, and flew out. Just as I was crossing the airstrip it began to snow.

I landed on time in Tampa in a blaze of sunlight and heat, and drove to my friend's home in Sarasota. Her son and his wife were there, but were leaving the next morning. "Sally," I said to my hostess' daughter-in-law, "do you have boots or galoshes?"

"Whatever for?" she asked.

"I think there's snow back home," I told her.

There was, inches of it; and she had no galoshes.

So it goes; what will happen to me this month I don't know; maybe I'll get to the hotel in good time and take off happily the next day. Maybe, delayed by a blizzard, I'll stagger in at four in the morning and not take off at all. I suppose, if I were younger, there would be an element of excitement about the uncertainty of weather. As it is, I no longer feel anything but apprehension and resignation.

March brings us as many varieties of weather as there are fingers on my hand. I like best the bright blue days when the puddles of yesterday's rain in the muddy roads reflect the sky and you go chasing around corners to look for spring, and perhaps meet snow. There are March evenings when the sky after sunset is lemon yellow or still the pale jade green of winter. And there are also dark days.

I recall a special day in autumn, last year, when the sky was charcoal and the rain fell in blowing sheets of water. Yet the trees, although their leaves were falling and blowing, scattering all over, had not lost all color and I knew that, given one moment of pure bright sunlight the entire landscape would be filled with sudden glory.

This is also true in March, however dark, though to be sure there are no autumn leaves. There are no leaves at all, but when the sun shines you have bits of sky caught in the prosaic puddles and the wind blows fresh and clean.

Whether I myself go south or not, my sister will be taking off for far countries. Last spring, it was to Venice and the Greek Islands. This year, Egypt, and wherever I am, I'll think of her in that old land, now striding forward, but still old. The only time I was there was in 1954 when I had breakfast in the old airport in Cairo and then flew on to Rome. So I haven't seen the pyramids, or ridden a camel, or drifted down the Nile, or answered the question of the Sphinx, who sits with her paws in the sand.

I really envy—though in a nice way—people who can plan, and be fairly sure the plans will materialize. Friends of mine took off the day after last Christmas for Africa, and I am sure nothing happened to alter their plans. I've learned the hard way, as I've often said, to make plans and accept the fact that they may not materialize. I used to wish desperately that I could see ahead, ten years—a year—even a month. Now I no longer yearn for an accurate crystal ball; an hour ahead is perhaps all I can reasonably ask.

March is the month when, thinking of lions and lambs, I recall the only time I ever saw baby lambs in profusion. That was in Australia back in 1939, on my first trip Down Under. I believe the month was July and that's their autumn.

In March, birthdays come to a number of people close to me. I plan for these ahead, in case I am away. If I'm not, the packages are in the library chest, wrapped and ready for mailing, or on order to be sent from the shops.

A granddaughter, born on my mother's birthday, will be seven in March. Her father would have been forty-one on the day after. There are many memorable birthdays this month, including one on March seventeenth—not St. Patrick's either.

Last March I was with this grandchild on her birthday; we had dinner out, and she had a lovely cake, erupting with sparklers that scared me more than they did her.

I am fully aware that it is the height of folly to trust a New England March. I've known days when it was so warm that flowers bloomed trustfully out of season and people went rushing out of wools into cottons, and even into shorts—heaven help them—yet a week later woke to find the silence of snow all around. This is a month of surprises; and I've not forgotten my mother's stories of the blizzard of '88. Not that we haven't had other blizzards since she was a schoolgirl, but in those days her particular city was not equipped to meet the crisis.

I suppose the only thing to do is to be prepared for anything; take the tweed coat, or even the old fur one; and the bulky sweater and the high warm boots; but also leave space for the light-weave suit, a cotton frock or two, and sandals. When I go south, I am armored for the occasional cold spell, so along with the cottons go the sweaters, the knit wool dress, and the suit I fly away in. This means twice as much luggage, of course, and when you travel, as I do, mostly by air, it can be inconvenient as well as expensive.

55

A year ago there were only three good hot beach days out of ten. Oh, sunshine, of course; but also cold and some rain and a sharp wind blowing. After that I traveled about one hundred and fifty miles to another part of the state where the thermometer sat relentlessly in the nineties and the humidity was beyond belief. And there I went one hot night to speak at a meeting for a friend and was seized, a few hours before, with the sort of virus which turns you green and rocks you on your feet. How I stayed on mine on the platform I never knew. And the next day, still slightly seasick, I drove many more long miles to still another part of the state and there we had fine walking and sight-seeing weather: cool, clear, sunny and windy; and at the motel where my daughter-in-law and I stayed for five days few ventured into the big swimming pool and those who did promptly turned indigo blue.

I suppose that somewhere on this earth there may be a perfect climate . . . not too hot or too cold; gentle warmth by day and a cooling breeze at night; where it rains only when you're asleep, enough for growth but not enough to interrupt your daytime plans. If there is such a spot, I've never found it. I don't think I'd really care to, for perfection can be monotonous and I hate monotony.

While my sister is in Egypt I wonder if she'll think of the beautiful garden she has created on Long Island. It was new last year when I was there in June; this year it will have grown and spread. It is a peaceful place, a place in which to meditate and to be quiet. Any of us who has a small patch of ground, a little bed of blossoms, begins, in March, to think of what will emerge in due time from the earth, even though in many districts the ground will still be snow-covered. But we know that under the snow or ice there is the softening, the stirring, the wonderful beginning again.

If this month I am to go walking on a white Florida beach, it may be warm or cool, but always there will be the Gulf to look at, and perhaps a decorative school of dolphin within sight. And I will stoop to the sand to hunt for unbroken shells, reminding myself that the ones which did not survive the storms, the pounding waters and the uncounted years, have been ground into infinitesimal particles to color the beaches.

Everything in nature is balanced. Often man upsets that balance and usually lives to regret it—but the fundamental balance remains and out of storm, stress, and devastation there comes the building of new beauty.

Easter is very early this year. I remember other early Easters when I insisted on wearing new suits and nearly froze to death. But whether the day is fair and warming up, or cold with an overcast sky and a sprinkling of snow, it is still Easter.

Each day relates itself to the one preceding it, and to the one ahead, yet each is in itself unique, a whole bright coin to squander or in memory, to hoard. Each is a fresh beginning. I am aware that on our calendar spring doesn't arrive until the twenty-first, but for me it starts as soon as our brief, and often violent, February has shaken herself free from the chains of ice and gone her way for another year.

All this past winter, I have watched my African violets bloom, rest, and bloom again. There's always at least one blossom somewhere among the plants on the battered table. I don't do anything for them except give them water and a northeast light. I'm not a gardener by nature, so I'm always amazed when anything blooms for me. When friends bring me books on the care and feeding of house plants, with definite instructions plus, perhaps, things to feed them with, I put them all carefully away. If I read the books, I'd give up. If I used the plant food, I'd be too lavish. Everything I've ever done has been wrong, according to the experts. Yet perhaps because I love the plants and often tell them so, they respond. All winter I've had the violets upstairs in the sunroom, with a begonia from a friend's outdoor garden, a little ivy plant, and a tall something, the name of which I don't know. There is also a gardenia, which is in its third year. It was in luxuriant bloom the Easter it came to me; last year it had about six blossoms, but I don't think it will have any this year. It stands on the chest, in the south window, with the sun on it, and I am careful to keep its feet wet for it loves water; and for the past two summers it's been out of doors, sheltered by a tall bush . . . The sunroom is a fine place in which to lie and read, look about, and see springtime even in winter. Downstairs in one huge wooden container there are two begonias, grown by Gussie, and forever flowering. One of these days they are going to grow right up through the living-room ceiling and try to get into the sunroom above. They have a fascination for me, rather like Jack's Beanstalk and I love the flowers which bloom, fall, and bloom again, wearing the shapes of dark pink hearts.

They remind me that springtime really begins in the human heart, no matter how wintery things have been; in spite of the ice-cold clutch of fear, the chilling reminder of grief, the ordinary day-by-day fatigue which clogs the wings of the mind like heavy snow, or the sensation which I often have of walking through the days and weeks, very delicately on terribly thin ice. But the heart's springtime still looks back to loveliness remembered, forward to happiness hoped for; and the sun within is that of the affection we give to others and receive from them; the inner light is the illumination of one's own citadel of spiritual security, a sort of conquering.

This past winter I scored one very mundane victory—I conquered the boiled egg. All the winter before I had wrestled with the problem. When I was young, I read innumerable English Victorian novels in many of which the hero, as a child, stood or sat by Papa at breakfast, while he sliced off the top of his morning egg and presented it to his son as a special treat. I'd never tried slicing off the tops of eggs myself, until a few summers ago when I observed my sister briskly attacking hers and then mine with one fell, calculated accurate swoop. She prefers to eat an egg from its shell.

When I tried this, if the egg didn't crash on the table or cascade up my sleeve, it blandly cracked down the middle, and oozing, just sat there looking at me. At which point, with admirable patience, my sister would remedy the matter.

But now I alone have triumphed. With the help of a timer I boil my egg and am no longer unsuccessful in "topping" it. I have learned to approach it boldly, striking a single blow without timidity; better attack than defense. But let me falter even for a moment and I'm in trouble.

That, perhaps, is the best way to approach any problem—swiftly, surely, boldly.

Not long ago someone asked me if I still went about stubbing my toes. She asked it tolerantly, even with concern. Well, of course, I do, not only literally but figuratively. When it's a literal stubbing, I can always blame it on something: someone moved the chair, or the rocker reached out to trip me, or I didn't know the step was there. But when it's a figurative stubbing, I've only myself to blame.

All of us stub our metaphorical toes over unexpected situations which we do not foresee, but which become obstacles that hurt us. When, occasionaly, we do learn to avoid one particular stumbling block, others usually crop up.

I daresay we learn more from what we consider our failures than from our achievements. We don't realize it at the time but, looking back, we recognize the lesson and, in the light of what we've learned, a failure may shine more brightly than a success.

Life, if fully lived, is never monotonous; there are always changes in the climate of the heart and mind, the good days and the bad, much like the vagaries of March. But they even up somehow, and while on a straight, quiet road there may be a sudden turn or hill, there is, from every hill, a view. Like March, living is full of astonishment and wonder.

One reason I like to go south in early March is that I can leave the snowbanks and the ice behind me and fly into an advanced spring—which also has tricks up her green sleeve. And though I may fly back again to more snowbanks, they won't last long, for the end of the month is really a northern spring's beginning.

Beginning? There is really no beginning to anything, nor ever an end, for life, living, and the seasons are circles, and one month drifts into another.

Even when the March sky is dark, we know in our hearts that there will soon be sun which will bring to the world about us

59

illumination and beauty. So it is perhaps, with personal problems which spread darkness all about us. It isn't easy to wait for the light, which is understanding and acceptance, but if we can do so, it will transfigure our private landscape. This inward light which can shine on the outer problem has a singular beauty, and we will be granted illumination which will help us solve difficulties or compromise with them.

I used to be very impatient with the compromise. I'm not any longer, for most of living is compromise. I don't mean compromise with rooted honesty and integrity but compromise in the sense of yielding somewhat, meeting others halfway, making the best of things.

March blows in and it will blow out. Lion or lamb? Who knows? Each has beauty.

Now people return from winter holidays, a little time of skiing or swimming, from cruises or flights. Others will go house hunting or start to think about boats laid up in marinas and the preparation of gardens. In this month, in this section of the country we are apt to tire a little; winter has sapped our vitality, and sometimes our spirits are low. But just around the next corner, there is April.

&ᘒ &᙭

"Lord, Thou hast given me a cell
Wherein to dwell
A little house whose humble roof
Is weather-proof;
Under the spars of which I lie
Both soft and dry . . ."

ROBERT HERRICK.

That is what Mr. Herrick wrote in "A Thanksgiving to God for His House." I copy it down, feeling as he felt some centuries ago. But, in climbing the thirteen steps to my bedroom, I do not visualize it as a cell but rather as a cloister, a withdrawing—place—all blue and white, with a pleasant mingling of woods, a bookcase filled with Chinese things and a very few books; an old lampstand with ivories on it, a Kwan Yin and a serene Madonna and her Child.

It is a quiet room, even when the dogs across the road bark, and as it is roughly the size of the study beneath, there are four windows, with a fifth in the small adjoining bathroom. The bedside lamps are of deep sapphire-blue glass; the parchment shades, pale blue with pastel mauve and pink shells, were painted for me by a friend. Nearby there is an old rocker, a Hotchkiss, the paint well worn; and underfoot, hooked rugs.

The big lamp on the dressing table is Delft and so are various other objects that are strewn about. The bulb in the big lamp is bright, but those by the bed are blue; for I very rarely read in bed at night.

The west wall has an exposed beam which runs into the bathroom. This is dark, old, and hand-hewn. It takes away, and properly, from the little-girl effect of the blue and white decor. For other color there are the mugs standing on recessed shelves, the etched bottles and the bits and pieces which, over the years have come to me through friends. On the bookshelf there's a moss-rose pitcher—there's lots of moss-rose-patterned china in the house: cups, saucers, even dessert plates; the mugs, a compote, a smaller pitcher, and a lamp. It is a design I'm fond of.

When we came here there grew in the neglected garden a living moss rose. They are hard to come by now, although a few nurseymen, notably one in California, stock them. I treasured mine, but over the years it has vanished, perhaps during a time when the garden was dug up and seeded to grass. We left only rose bushes, but somehow the moss rose disappeared.

No windows face me as I wake in this room; they are in back of me or to my left. So there's no view until I get up and go to a window to observe a faint dawn flush, or the full sun and the birds at the feeder. Usually, if it's early enough, there are pheasant on the ground, and the hens, heavy as they are, sometimes fly up onto the feeding shelf. Last January, after the heavy snowfall, I saw a cock pheasant brilliant against the snow. He had scooped out a place for himself and was industriously seeking seeds which were on the earth he had bared.

In this room I admire my pale blue telephone, light in the hand which, when I lift the transmitter, is illuminated. I have sometimes used it as a night table. Lying in bed with the lamps still on I can see any number of things—on the recessed shelves, on the bookshelves—which have a meaning for me far beyond the china, or porcelain, ironstone or crystal from which they were fashioned.

At night, if I go upstairs early, it is usually to the sunroom where I can admire the violets. Their leaves have yellowed in the past month—am I giving them to much water? I may lie on the couch to read awhile by the old lamp with an owl painted on the base; or turning out that light and switching on the one over the television set, which casts its small but sufficient light upward, I sit in a vast, shabby upholstered rocking chair and look at the screen.

When in the sunroom the lights are out, and I go into the bedroom, it is to make myself ready for sleep and to lie awhile in the pleasant darkness with the west windows open to think of the day just past and the one which is to come.

There are always sounds in old houses: the stairs creak as if a foot had been set upon the treads; the furniture makes sudden sharp noises. These I like. They do not cause me any ill ease. They are part of the house which surrounds me, and all the sounds are reassuring and friendly.

The bedroom is in effect a boudoir, in which I do not (often) sulk. (The word boudoir came, I understand, from the French verb meaning to sulk.)

Properly speaking, a boudoir is not a bedroom. In the days of boudoirs it was, I imagine, a small resting place, perhaps a dressing room (though I cannot fancy sulking in a dressing room). But in this time and place I think of the boudoir as the bedroom itself.

It is a room in which there is peace. Even on those days and nights when there is no peace within me, or I cannot yet reach out and find it, it is all around me.

When guests have gone, when the downstairs and outside lights are turned off, when I have finished a book or watched the news, then I come into the blue and white room. A little later, in the darkness, I give thanks for the bygone day, and put my trust in the day to which I shall, for a while yet, waken; usually to the speech of birds, even in winter.

I cannot state as firmly as Mr. Herrick that this humble roof is always weatherproof . . . but it is proof I believe against the weather I make for myself, gales of anxiety and falling rain of tears. And so, I give thanks that in this particular cell I live and move and have my being.

April

When I open the door to April, I never know what I'll find on the stone steps, kitten or wild cat. Sometimes she appears with frail, early flowers in one hand, a wreath of starflake snow in her yellow hair, wearing galoshes and carrying an umbrella.

Last year on the eighth day she wore a full moon, slanted across her forehead, and on the twenty-third, the silver crescent of the new. Last year, she brought us Easter.

This year she is adorned by the argent crescents quarters and crown on different dates and this year she does not bring us Easter . . . perhaps that will make her shed some cool, bright tears, or even sulk a little (I can recommend a special boudoir for her).

I think of April as slender and light on her little green feet, and I fancy that her face is heart-shaped, and that her eyes alter from blue to gray according to her mood; maybe with a green or hazel glint here and there. I'm sure her hair is also as much pale green as it is yellow—perhaps the color of the spring leaves on the willows. But what she wears in her hair can be anything: glistening raindrops or a cluster of stars when no moon shows?

Last year, as I recall, dire prophecies were made of coming

64

April storms, but I can't remember whether or not these came true. But every storm must pass and not even a late howling blizzard can keep April from her annual duties, the spring house-cleaning, the growth, the promise and fulfillment.

Thus is a capricious month, but sometimes the unexpected is fun. A middle-of-the-road attitude is practical, I think, so I'll listen, with held breath, for the silver chiming of the peepers, and keep my snow boots handy.

Now the April birthdays come along. When my sister was born, I was banished to the home of friends to await the event. I think I may often have written of my dark disappointment, for when my father said that I was to have a surprise in the spring I figured it had to be a pony. Where he would have kept a pony in our city I've no idea. But eventually I was happy that my gift was a little girl named Esther and that we were able to keep her. Being premature and weighing in at around three pounds at a time when the medical profession was without today's facilities, that happy outcome was at first doubtful.

I'm glad she was born, and that Gladys Taber also was, in this month, as well as my twins, and the close friend who is also my agent; and a number of other friends.

This month I must reluctantly take up my occasional speaking in public again. In private, I just talk and talk and have been doing so (or my parents so contended) since I was ten months old.

For the past two winters I've done little speaking during the bad months. Last January I made one terrified trip to New York, and the weather was fine; I had two nearby engagements in February, and the less said about driving conditions then the better. But the older I grow, the more I fret about winter transportation. I still recall one time when I had only a short distance to go, but all of it was over ice. I was quite conscious of the fact that I was to speak for what is known as a Good Cause, so it seemed unjust that it had to be so difficult to get to the dinner and back. I'm certain my own personal cause would have been lost if it hadn't been for a wonderful driver-escort and his practically unbeatable four-wheel-drive car. But I was grateful beyond words to walk into this house that night with life and limbs intact.

Have you ever found that sometimes when you perform what you believe to be a service or kindness, obstacles and frustrations are often your immediate rewards?

One autumn evening, when the pastor of my church had driven considerable distance to help another small church raise some greatly needed funds, his car sank deeply and firmly in the mud of what was the only parking space. One of the friends with him had to go and hunt for a tow car. And his only consolation—because it made him laugh—was a passing woman who remarked, "Haven't you noticed that when you try to do something good everything goes wrong?"

Well, that's a sweeping statement but, a while later, hearing of an enormous and destitute family I depleted my sweater stock and my shoe closet and gave the bundle to a friend to deliver in another state. Then I went out feeling slightly noble, as if my halo had just been repolished, and returned home to find plumbers whacking away in the cellar at a broken hot-water pipe.

Oh, well, I've often thought—and said—that to expect reward for a kindness, whether spontaneous or calculated, is unrealistic; it is absurd. If virtue is its own reward, so must kindness be.

Also, I've stated, and I believe it more each year, that it is just as well not to inquire into one's motives for doing or giving—you can so easily come up with answers that spell ego, vanity, or the wish to be praised. Long ago, a wise man told me that the motive doesn't really matter. He said, "You drop the seed . . . it doesn't make any difference, really, *why* you do so . . . the seed is the important thing."

So it is. You may look in vain (and usually do) for the bread cast upon the waters to return in the shape of a cake with many layers and bright with candles. You may sit quietly waiting for gratitude to pour over you like April sunshine, and if you sit long enough, you'll have to turn on the house lights, for otherwise you'll be in the dark. But if a giver receives no benefit except the growth of his own generous spirit, the taker surely does. A seed can grow into just about anything . . . a tree perhaps, which

66

can provide sustaining fruit and shade from pitiless heat. But you can't expect that same seed to extend itself and suddenly grow masses of orchids just for you.

Giving is never a one-way street. Perhaps sometime someone will do us an enormous and unexpected favor and we won't connect it with the favor we did someone else, casually, long ago. Yet there could be a connection.

A number of times in my life I've been saved by the clear, lovely bell of kindness not rung by anyone for whom I'd ever done anything. No, the bell just rang out of the blue; out of the nowhere, almost, these things have come to me. And I'm sure to us all if only we'd stop and look back to wonder: Why did that happen when and as it did? Perhaps the seed grew orchids, after all, a year, two years or ten later.

It is sometimes said that the world owes us a living. I don't believe it. I think we have to work for it and sometimes even when we do work, it isn't forthcoming, or not as we'd hoped. And I don't believe anyone owes us gratitude. Often it comes to us spontaneously and sincerely; often not. But it isn't *owed*. If we ourselves are able to give it in return for all that's been bestowed upon us, so much the better. If we do not receive it from others, what of it?

I'm afraid we expect too much from life and from people, whether close to us or strangers, and expect too much from love and our own compassionate impulses. The only reliable source upon which we can wholly depend and from Whom we can expect exactly what we have earned, is God. He knows; He balances the accounts and His is an impartial all-comprehending justice.

Hundreds of people will not agree with me and upon occasion I haven't agreed with myself; yet I'm certain it's true.

A year ago this month we planted my Faith tree outdoors. It had been given to me just before the previous Christmas by my friends Rita and Bill and came in a small square wooden container with instructions on how to treat it as a house plant.

Sun and water, said the little booklet that came with it. I had just one free window ledge wide enough, and away from the heat. It is in the study and faces south, so all that winter, until the frost went from the ground the Faith tree lived there. It had been amply fed before leaving the nursery and I watched it to see if it would grow.

When it went outdoors, we put it on the edge of a field (where the lawn mowers wouldn't run over it) and marked it with red stakes, because given strength and good fortune, the tiny evergreen with the long Latin name could grow as high as ten feet and reach, also, considerable girth.

The Faith tree wasn't named for me. I could, if I wanted to, go and fetch the little booklet and copy out the impressive real name, but I do not feel so inclined. It's hardy, and it has the azure haze of a blue spruce (which it isn't), but the nursery people who grow it have a personal interest and pride in it, and affection for it. And because they believe in the future and know, as they say in the booklet, that "without Faith there is no future," they call it the Faith tree.

We had a bad drought last summer. The little tree was well watered weekly and sometimes in between, and it grew. During this winter, I think in December, when we had a clear or melting spell, we discovered we could see it from the living-room windows. Then came January's first storm and, of course, we could not even see the stakes.

I waited with some apprehension for the snow to melt and when it did, there was the Faith tree. I haven't gone down to measure it, but I am willing to swear it's grown some more, having been nourished, and not murdered, by the snow.

Faith needs nourishment; it requires not only sunshine but storm; sunshine heartens, but storm strengthens if you can accept and withstand it.

My faith has been sorely tried at times, in which I'm no different from the vast majority of people . . . but, except for one black period long ago, which lasted for some months, it

68

has never failed me for more than a few minutes or hours at a time.

Occasionally people write me in despair and desperation; they have lost everything, they tell me, including faith. What are they to do about it?

These letters are very difficult to answer because there is no formula. Many have been suggested, but they don't all work for everyone. And you can't, with a good conscience, reply in terms of clichés, banalities, generalities, with your pen or typewriter ribbon immersed in inky soothing syrup. Emergence from darkness into light is a personal victory; how you accomplish it is up to you. You have, of course, if you look for it, help from people who love you. But the ultimate conquering is your own affair. One person's way of solving a problem might not be your way or mine.

There are, in Australia, mines where the brown coal is on the surface, though most mines are underground. I think of one's personal faith as a mine, sometimes on the surface, open to the sun and yielding readily the material for warmth and comfort; at other times underground, far in the depths of one's personal self, tunneled deep and dimly lighted; sometimes not lighted at all. Then you have to dig for it.

Faith is a hard core of inner sustenance. It is a tall tree with tremendous, deep roots. It is the house in which we live. Sometimes the core is hard to find; sometimes the tree is shaken with wind or struck by lightning; and sometimes we forget or mislay the key to the house. But faith is an attitude of mind, a quality of heart, and a spiritual benefaction. Without it we are homeless, destroyed, and starved.

Faith can be weakened by dwelling on past errors and unhappiness; it can be made stronger by the present struggle, and always it can join hands with its little sister, Hope, looking toward the future.

It was kind of my parents to name me Faith; it has given me something to try to live up to, although for many years I did not recognize this challenge.

69

It costs me something to admit that, even now, I fall easily into the dreamy state known as wishful thinking. This is not faith—it isn't even a close relative of Hope; perhaps a second cousin once removed? And I know better than to think wishfully. I know I can't sit with my hands folded and wish myself into better situations or solutions, or wish myself out of certain circumstances. For these alterations I must work, and while I am working, although I can draw courage from hope, I must depend upon faith.

You'd be astounded perhaps if I were to tell you how many people who write me want to be something they are not—doctors, lawyers, painters, actors, writers—or just rich in this world's temporal goods. But they won't become anything by wishing; they have to work. Any profession or trade requires training and work; and as for wealth there is seldom pie in the sky, and few people, except through legacies or the winning of some extraordinary prize, receive an overflowing silver platter heaped with fruits for which they haven't worked; fruits they haven't seeded, tended, and reaped.

The extraordinary, exacting, unrelenting discipline of life and living demand sacrifice, self-abnegation, and labor; but the rewards can be bountiful.

I had a son who, early in his life, thought he wanted to be a physician. One night, when he was on his way out to a party, I asked him how many parties he'd be willing to refuse. He hadn't thought of that, or of the long hard years of study and preparation, or of the fact once he had reached his goal, nine nights out of ten he'd be taken away from a pleasant social gathering, or his family life by the demands of his profession.

A sensible child, he decided that the life of a medical man was not for him. I thought of him a good deal last year while I was writing a novel about a doctor.

My son didn't really want his dream enough to make it a reality by working for it; so he went on to other things. I was somewhat sorry that he didn't follow through, just as I was when my younger son decided not to become a clergyman, which was, during the Second World War, his ambition. I've often thought I'd like four sons in the professions: doctor, lawyer, teacher, clergyman. But I had only two and each outgrew his early dream. Perhaps some of the grandchildren will become one or the other, or make their marks in all the professions, I've mentioned. I'd like a scientist in the family, too, and there are many grandchildren.

But they, like the rest of us, will gain nothing by wishful thinking or through pleasant daydreams . . . whatever they accomplish, in whatever field, must be through work, dedication, and faith.

This spring many of us will make gardens and—if we seriously work at gardening—will see blossom and fruit in season.

This year the almanac again predicts weather breeders and lots of rain. Well, we need rain and whatever April's whims, I do not intend to quarrel with her, any more than you'd bicker with someone you love, who has come to visit you after a year-long absence, and who upsets your household, perhaps by tracking mud into the halls and on the carpet, or forgetting to close doors and windows, or deciding to go off on private expeditions without telling you she won't be home for lunch.

I'm hoping for rain and sun, for everyone's gardens, and especially for my Faith tree and for the roses which, promised me last Christmas, will arrive in time for planting.

I do not suppose I'll live to see my Faith tree grow ten feet high. I know I feel ten feet high when I go out and look at it, walking toward the edge of the field in snow, or mud, or on bare dry ground, and thinking about its quiet struggle to survive and grow.

I hope it reaches its full height and breadth and lives out its allotted years of sun and storm, darkness and light, rain and drought, cold and heat in triumph—as a rooted Faith must always do.

For I'm as sure of what faith can do as I am that April—willful and generous, capricious and kind—will slip gently into May.

71

"Peace be to this house."

ST. LUKE, 10: 5

In talking about the room which leads out of my bedroom to the double guest room, I never know whether to call it a sun porch or a sunroom. I suppose it's a sunroom.

There isn't much wall space. To the right of my bedroom door as you come into the sunroom there's a television set and enough space above it to hang the enlarged photograph of my husband as a very young man, standing beside his first airplane, during World War One. To the left there's a small closet in which I hang blouses, while on the shelf at top there's practically anything I don't know what to do with. In the brief wall space before you come to the guest-room door there's a little electric icebox.

There's no space on the south. That's one continuous wall of casement windows, with blinds you can let down when the sun's too bright. At the far end where the mulberry tree looks in, there's a Navy chest with plants on it; it is water-stained as is anything upon which I set plants. It would take a craftsman half a lifetime to refinish the chest, the sunroom table, and the desk in the living room.

The east side of the porch is also a wall of casement windows, shorter than the other. There's a couch bed there heaped with pillows—one in crewel work made for me by a friend (as was one downstairs), and to the right of the couch stands the solid wood card table which was my mother's, where the violets live. A reading lamp's there, the one with the owl on it. After that you come back to guest-room door and that completes the tour.

Over the violet table there's a painting which was done by the daughter of friends. It's of a wide and lazy river, the banks thick with trees, the sky infinitely blue. This is a painting which

72

rests you if you look at it awhile, and you find you're drifting downriver.

The guest-room door is kept open by a magazine stand filled with old magazines of an erudite nature. I've never known what to do with them. Oh, and over the icebox there's another friend's painting; this one is of the view from the window of the little house on Cape Cod in which I spent two and a half summers.

That's it, except for two narrow glass tables by the south window and three chairs: a sort of iron reclining chair apt to fall down, and with a cushion that is disintegrating—I must do something about that someday; the big upholstered rocker if you take the cushion out of that you'll find anything—a dime, which is nice; cracker crumbs, which aren't; even a peanut shell or two. The other chair is of the small television type.

Occasionally I go up there in the daytime and lie down with a book, or sometimes sleep a little. Evenings, alone, I read or watch television. Often, daytimes I watch the birds, restless and intent, on the bare or leafed-out branches of the mulberry or a squirrel scampering up the enormous trunk. Mostly, I let the singular peace of this room sink into my blood and bones as the sun does when you're on a beach, though peace is in the sunroom even on dark days or windy and stormy ones. It is not disturbed by swirling snow or rain lashing in from the south or southeast.

It's a warm room; when I came here to live it was unheated, but we remedied that. I have upon occasion, when my furnace has decided to quit—usually over a weekend and almost always when the weather is zero—dressed close to the south windows where, if there was sun, a thermometer, set on a table or the chest, would run right up to eighty.

It is a room in which to reflect, contemplate, or fall into a half sleep; the sort of room which is perfect for the quiet time and the do-nothing time. A nice room in which, if you can't compose yourself to slumber or meditation, and neither book nor television beckon, you can sit in the rocker, which has a way of walking if you rock, and do cross-word puzzles.

Gladys Taber and I do them on the Cape. At least she does, but now and then she permits me to fill in a word, which usually she erases, as she's much better at this pastime than I am. I think I can hold my own with her when it comes to jigsaw puzzles. Last year, when I despaired of ever getting the hard words in the Sunday newspaper puzzles, I bought myself a book with the solutions in the back and quite frankly cheated when I was overcome with frustration.

I was, of course, cheating no one save myself.

As a matter of fact, when we do cheat, we may think we're cheating others, but in the last analysis, it's always ourselves, whether at cross words, solitaire, or something really important.

We cheat ourselves of many things; often of joy, and many times—by evasion—of facing an issue, which is a wonderful exercise in self-discipline; and too many times, by not saying the right words to someone, bringing them a little comfort or hope or just the knowledge that someone cares, we cheat ourselves far more than we cheat them.

This morning I woke early to a most beautiful sunrise. I have been gladdened all autumn, winter, and spring by the sunsets. I don't often see the sun rise, but this morning the eastern sky was a dull deep blaze of dark rose. I should rise early more often and not cheat myself of this.

May

This is a more predictable month than most although my sister's May wedding day was hotter than July. I remember how ill I was, yet I managed to be matron of honor done up in ruffles and a big hat, and after the reception took to my bed while everyone else—but everyone—exclusive of the bride and groom—went on to a spontaneous sort of party instigated by my father. I also recall that in the country in June of that same year the furnace stayed on and fireplaces were bright with flames.

So perhaps no month's predictable.

Maybe someone will hang a May basket at my door; maybe not; come to think of it, why don't I arrange one for myself? A little basket with a tin lining, filled with water and crowded with the tiny pink fists of crab-apple blossoms.

I haven't been south in the spring for a long time. I am thinking of the nearby south, Maryland, Virginia but they're way ahead of us. Once, outside of Washington, D.C., I heard peepers long before they rang their bells in my state, and another time in Williamsburg in April everything was exploding into bloom and the mockingbirds sang all night. I had expected to go back to Williamsburg last month with my sister and was sorry I could not, for I haven't seen it for years. And I haven't seen the cherry trees blossom in Washington for even longer.

Once, in the early nineteen thirties, when I went with a friend who was visiting us from the North, it rained like crazy all the time we were sight-seeing in the Capital and the only cherry blossoms we saw were sent to us by my friend's sister, who was holding the fort at home. These came from a florist, in a huge box with the explanation that this way we'd be sure to see some. We came back to New York a little while later to our own botanical gardens in Brooklyn, where cherry blossoms bloomed in wonderful profusion.

Now I have cherry trees here, gracefully weeping pink tears.

In this month my youngest nephew was born, as was his sister. During the soft May springtime I would like to go to Arlington Cemetery to which he came in 1950 from Korea. Perhaps the apple blossoms blow white and the tulips grow. Perhaps, too, Bruce's simple marker is not far from that of a later Commander-in-Chief than his.

This month we'll be able to tell whether the autumn planting resisted moles as well as frost. It did last year. I once had a gardener who planted a mothball with each bulb and the friend who now does my small planting for me beneath the south windows and along the brick path border said that his forebears used a clove of garlic so last fall we tried both, and all winter I wondered anxiously if I'd get mothball trees and garlic shrubs instead of flowers. But everything came up tulips and daffodils and scylla and narcissus. Perhaps this year the moles have decided they like the flowers.

Recently I was thinking about Germany, which I first saw in the spring of nineteen fourteen. I remember May there and the flowering trees along a canal. But most of all I remember my mother's friend with whom I lived: beautiful, gay, witty, and with a most marvelous sense of dignity. Half German and half English, she was extremely practical and could cook superbly. Her book of recipes, handwritten, came from all over the world.

76

She did not cook while I lived with her, but I saw the book and I heard about the cooking school she'd gone to. I went to one myself in Berlin, but it didn't take nor did her talent rub off on me.

Born a noblewoman, she was one in every sense of the word throughout her entire life, in sickness and in health, in poverty and prosperity.

I have a number of friends who set great store by ancestry (unless it's the kind you don't talk about . . . like a horse thief hanging from the family tree) and certainly to possess ancestral inheritance is marvelous, providing it consists of the inherited genes—or whatever they are—of integrity and goodness and intelligence. All the rest, as far as I am concerned, doesn't count . . . I mean the crowns, tiaras, diadems, baubles, and trinkets, on a cherished family tree, rather like left-over Christmas trimmings.

Ah, but the solid traits, the good. If these have been passed on down—and if we have taken care of them—how fortunate we are, no matter what has been the social status of our forebears!

There are still monarchies, of course, where titles descend from generation to generation; some are still bestowed for achievement in many fields or for great philanthropy. But the majority of nations no longer give titles or even acknowledge them, although they're still used by courtesy and seem especially decorative when the holder, owner, or wearer comes over here. We are a republic, a democratic nation, or so we think, yet many of us still figuratively—and sometimes even literally—bend the knee to the ancient or not so ancient, title. And we have a few of our own, although of different kind and not descending to the next generation; the doctorates, for instance, are earned through applications to higher education; some are given as honorary degrees; and then we have our judges and government officials.

I often think of the little crowns which members of the German nobility were entitled to use . . . embroidered on lingerie, set upon handbags, framed over fireplaces, or painted on porcelain. I have seen many a five-pointed crown, and also, nine, and I have one piece of crown-engraved silver, a tea caddy made in about 1800 which belonged to my mother's friend with whom I lived in Germany. I called her Tante. The little silver box, which has a very remarkable and romantic story back of it, was not her own family's, but belonged to the delightful woman who was her foster mother.

I had other pieces of flat silver which were Tante's and which I've since given to my children. And a massive punch-bowl ladle, which almost broke my wrist to lift, went to a friend who often entertained large groups in the old manner.

As far as titles are concerned it seems to me that we are all, whatever our inheritances, children of one Father. He does not consult *Burke's Peerage*, or the *Social Register* or *Who's Who*. What must count with Him is what we are fundamentally and what we make of our particular inheritances—what we become. And becoming anything at all, for better or worse, is not an overnight process; it requires long and continuous effort.

Perhaps we all manufacture our own little crowns with as many points as, over a lifetime, we can hammer out—integrity, love, giving, sharing, compassion, understanding. Sometimes we don't succeed in fashioning much of anything or else the circlet is beaten into curious shapes by the sledge hammers of our own failures, but at least we can try.

Young May, the year's debutante, wears a crown of blossoms as she dances through the fields and by the streams, or tiptoes on the sand, or climbs a mountain; as she travels down country roads and city streets. She knows that she did not create her beauty without help, for each month contributes something to the next. Winter's snow and sleet, ice and frost, all contained nourishment, without which there would be no blossoms. So May, too, has ancestry.

Everything which comes to us has within it the seeds of growth. Troubles sometimes seem to me like snowballs which we shape ourselves; sometimes soft and quickly dissipated; but often hard, ice-cold, and hurtful. When understanding, like a warm wind, or

78

a steady radiation of sunlight, melts the ice, there is, as in the springtime, the going forward, the growing.

In what are now thought of as the old days—and I sometimes hear from teenagers who refer to "your generation" or "your times" or "your era" as if I'd flourished in a covered wagon—I did a good deal of countryside snooping, because I was able to drive—or rather be driven—about during the clement months of spring, summer, and autumn. So for a number of years, I knew almost every part of this state, and a good deal of the bordering states, in their spring dress. Now, except for summer driving to Cape Cod or Long Island, I rarely travel more than twenty-odd miles by car—and only very occasionally just to look. Usually I'm going somewhere: to church, to shop, or to have dinner with friends.

I was fortunate, I suppose, that the days of the long drives past brooks, rivers, and beaches and into the hills, almost always on winding roads, took place when there was not the present congestion of innumerable cars on the big throughways for there was time then to poke about, to see and to examine and to stop somewhere new or familiar for tea or lunch.

I don't like to do things by halves, so I have two favorite months—May and October.

May is all lilacs and dogwood and pear trees and apple blossoms, all valley lilies and tulips—and also, if my recollection is correct, dandelions. It is all the wide blue wonder of a springtime sky. May, bringing to full bloom the buds of April, crowns herself with her own scented glory.

Sometime I'd like to spend May on Cape Cod and see the beach plum in blossom; I'd also like to spend one May in London. Yet May at home is so seductive I'd be sorry to miss what she offers.

This is the month of my father's birthday. I wonder what it was like in China in that distant May of 1864?

It is curious to ponder that, were he alive upon this earth, he'd be a century old. He died, however, a long time ago; and it seems

79

strange to be over a decade older now than my father was when he went away, leaving me here.

Now is the time when the sown seed emerges and the bulbs thrust slender green lances upward and the fruit trees are a constant miracle of color and faint scent. Forsythia has been with us for quite a while in and out of the house, cascading in gold, a yellow storm. But lilacs—these I brood over from the time of the first tight, hard, dark buds, through the expansion and the color.

From one year to the next I never remember if it's May that brings us dogwood in bloom or June! But I know, in May, the year is marching toward roses.

Everything goes forward; nothing is static. The human spirit also shares this instinctive integral forward-march of nature; it is obstructed only by the drag, the hesitance and heaviness, the reluctance of the human mind and body. No one can constructively live in the past, or realistically exist upon the dream of the future. The time is always now. Today is Thursday. Tomorrow will be Friday, but when I wake to the calling of birds, the drum of rain, or the sunlight slanted along the floor, it will not be tomorrow . . . but today.

Recently, a friend said to me that only when her own life became altered in many ways did she realize that alteration is a part of living. "You know," she added, "you can't remain in one physical position long; you have to rise from your chair, you have to change your posture; even in your sleep you shift positions, or you hurt somewhere; and living's like that." She then told me something which I cherish which was that when she and her family had to move unexpectedly from this state to another, someone remarked to her three-year-old boy, "Now, you have no home."

"Oh, yes," he said confidently, "we have a home—we just have to find a house to put it in!"

Think about that if you are moving this spring, or next fall, or anytime for that matter. For what the child said is a profound truth; wherever we are, wherever we must go, we carry with us the spiritual home we have built of love and warmth, of lessons learned, and of memories and hopes. All we have to do is find a house in which to install them. Sometimes it's a bigger house than the one we have had to leave, sometimes smaller, sometimes just a handful of rooms or even only one. But whatever it is, it's waiting for us to come in and establish a home.

Stone walls do not a prison make; neither does a roof and four walls make a home. I've been in beautiful houses which gave me no sense that they were homes. They were doors, windows, roofs, eaves, and walls dividing space into rooms. Perhaps the inhabitants had not brought a home with them, only furniture and draperies, china, silver, and bric-a-brac.

Most of us have, of course, lived in more than one house. There are many young people nowadays continually on the move for business reasons. One girl told me, a while back, that in nine years of marriage she'd moved seven times. Well, no matter how many houses we have lived in, we are fortunate if each has been, for however long our tenancy, a home in the true sense.

Now, in May, is the time people go looking for new—or old— dwellings, for bigger or smaller apartments, for a place with trees and room for a garden, or for a flat on top of a tall building with a view over water or a park. Now, too, is the time when both men and women are busy weekends, making their boats shipshape, big boats, little ones. Everyone seems to have some kind of boat these days. I have seen them being moved along the highways, miles and miles from any stretch of water, but eventually, I know, they'll wind up on a river or a lake, on the Sound or a bay.

I know people who bring to the comparatively short season they spend in navigating their boats—vacations, weekends—more enthusiasm than they bestow upon their houses. For them, a boat— cruising, sailing, or anchored in a quiet port for the night— is home.

It's exciting to rent, or buy a house in the spring but perhaps even more so in winter, or autumn, for then you don't know what you can expect. Oh, the owner will tell you, and you may recognize the shapes of certain trees and bushes. But you do not know all the secrets. Some, of course, can be disturbing, as, for instance, when you find, after you move in, that *you* need a new

81

heating system (as I've done); or that the house had put its best foot forward while you were looking at it, and only after you've moved do you discover it has another and shabbier foot—one over which you and your budget are bound to trip.

The house in which I live is old, as you know; it is certainly falling down here and there and I'm sure you understand my trepidation about the plaster. Almost every day I discover peeling paint, or a bit of wallpaper looking fragile, or a fine hairline crack where I'm sure one had not been the day before. We certainly stand in need of redecorating. I keep putting it off for one reason or another. I tell myself, hopefully, that when I no longer need this house and when it no longer needs me, the new owners will want their own redecoration. Someday, though, I'll have to come to it and I shudder to think of the welter and confusion.

I have lived here for almost thirteen years and since the raw March day when I was first taken to see this house, I knew it was home. We didn't move in until August, but we used to come over in the spring and look to see what we'd be having during the next spring. I remember coming in May and seeing old, bent apple trees and big dogwoods, and later finding in the most unexpected places more dogwoods which needed to be stripped of vines and also discovering cork bushes all about, even growing out of stone walls. Everything I found in those first spring visits and during the summer and autumn and on to the next spring, was newly discovered treasure.

Violets in the grass, little ones, crouching close to the ground; wild flowers and spring beauty in the fields; and, as summer advanced, all the wild flowers including butterfly weed, which is the loveliest, I think. I also remember, at the other house, the first summer we were there, discovering cardinal flowers in great profusion, looking like a five-alarm fire, along the banks of the brook.

So now here we are and it's May again. There's not much left of the apple trees, but as long as there's a blossom they'll be left there, with their few thick twisted branches. But the dogwoods have grown and grown . . . all are white save one; and all, save that one, native to the piece of land upon which they grew. Until I saw them first in blossom I hadn't realized how many shades of white there are.

I like to think that I have gone forward a little, grown with the dogwoods, and made, out of the materials of myself, this home.

❦ ❦

"Pleasantest
Of all ties is the tie of host and guest."

AESCHYLUS

Well, I'm not so sure that the Greeks had hard and fast valid words for it. I'm certain I've distressed many a host and hostess, in my time. As for guests, in this house, there have been a great many, usually just at dinner time; but some for overnight, for a weekend or longer. With some exceptions, these have been my children, but they have come to me from as far away as Hawaii, England, and Australia.

My parents had more summer guests than I can count in the years of Hilo Farm on Shelter Island, and my sister and I added our quota of young people. There seemed always be to be room and, in those distant days, domestic assistance. Mother had a gift for making people comfortable: writing paper in the guest rooms, stamps, toothbrushes in cupboards, paste, and all the little things one needs for the unexpected overnighter.

This custom she passed down to me, almost as a compulsion. To be sure, I keep the guest paper and stamps in the living-room desk along with elastic bands, paper clips, pens, and transparent tape, and when the guests depart I seize upon these articles for my own use.

Mother's guest rooms—and for years there were only two; later, three—were kept exclusively for the people who stayed with

83

us; clothes closets and bureau drawers were empty. I admit that nowadays I often spread out all over the house, it being too much trouble, for instance, to banish summer clothes to the attic. But when someone is expected, I hastily clean out the dresser where I'm apt to keep knitted dresses, and the closets, see to it that there are hangers and check the bath oil, soap, towels, razors, toothbrushes, paste, headache tablets and the like.

The double guest room which you enter from the sunroom or the hall, shares with the single guest room a big bath off the hall. It has two windows to the east and a small one, north. And the half asleep guests or guest can, in this room, look down the slope to dogwoods and apple trees and to the little pond. A summer sojourner is not apt to see any water in the pond.

My guest from Hawaii who was here one spring—we spent part of the time in New York—filled the downstairs rooms with flowers; I had to be absent for a short time, so she took a taxi and went shopping. I returned to find her arranging flowers—she's an expert—and complaining. She could walk out of her house on Maui and just cut; or if she bought any of the flowers with which the Islands abound, the bill came, of course, to a fraction of the sum one would expend here.

That's another thing my mother always did; put flowers in all guest rooms. I try to do this, too, just a bloom or two, if out of season; or a larger vase of whatever has consented to grow around this place.

In my parents' summer home there were no rules except the ones concerning meal hours—and my father sometimes violated those. Here, we are a little more routine-minded.

I feel that anyone who stays with someone else for any length of time needs privacy, and I try to give it to them. After all, I have an excuse if one is needed: I have to work. So my guests have time to take naps, read, go walking about the place if the weather permits, do my cross-word puzzles, write letters, or just sit and think. One of my Australian guests, a young nurse, who was with me for a time last July and again in September, got her letter writing done, and also took frequent naps. She had for her own that part of the house which is away from every other part and she was quieter than any mouse I've ever known. I told her when she was coming in September that I couldn't whirl her around as much as I had in July, because I was working against a deadline. After that I was afraid *not* to work lest she miss the sound of typing in the study and think me a prevaricator. I believe I accomplished more during the week she was here than in several weeks before. She was a newspaper addict; give her two or three newspapers daily, and she read the print right off them. She's in London now and misses our newspapers, so I send her clippings.

Funny thing, but when you meet someone and mention it to someone else, the reaction always is, "What's she like?" if it's a woman. Or if you have a guest coming from far away, your friends ask the same question.

How do you answer it? What is anyone "like"? You can tell them height, weight, age, occupation, nationailty, residence and interests—but, what else?

It's rather like filling out a form or a questionnaire. The facts, the salient points, yes; but the real person, no.

The reason you can't tell anyone one hundred per cent what anyone else is like is that you know only what they're like in relation to yourself.

So, I'm myself. I have relatives, I have friends; to each of them I mean something different: they may agree on the outward things, but probably not on the inward; for all people are like icebergs, the greater part of them being submerged. What I am to, say, one of my friends or children is not what I am to another.

It's the same with us all. Therefore, if you ask me about so-and-so who will shortly occupy your double guest room, I cannot tell you what she is like except, so to speak, the vital statistics.

And should you be interested enough to wonder and ask me what I'm like, I can't tell you that either; I don't know. I think we see ourselves, most often, through the eyes of others; and it is pretty confusing when those eyes, even if they have twenty-twenty vision, do not see the same image.

85

But I hope that whoever comes here to occupy for a short or longer space the double guest room looking toward the sunrise and with the little north window back of the old twin beds— one bed really at one time, but now cut into two, losing the antique value but very practical—I hope they'll be happy here *whatever* they are like.

June

Now the year slips into its most romantic phase. Where April hesitates, and May promises, June fulfills. Everyone who comes calling on you in June—at least in this part of the world—should leave a rose as a calling card. For June is the door which swings open upon summer, azure skies, long sunlight, vacations, and birdsong.

It has been nesting time since last month and the birds are busy about their building. I miss some of them. I haven't seen an oriole on this place for years, nor a blue bird, although I saw one, on the road, Thanksgiving day.

Now is the month of the courting songs, even, perhaps torch songs; the time of matins, also of vespers. Next month they'll be busy raising families; and the month after it will be so hot that they'll hide in the woods, and you'll hear them mostly at dawn and sunset.

We have no mockingbirds here, although I understand they've been seen in New England. The only ones I've met were in Virginia and Arizona. We do have catbirds and thrashers who can, and do, imitate the calls and songs of other birds. I sometimes think that one of my frustrations is that I've never heard a nightingale except long ago on a radio program recorded, I suppose, in England.

To me, birdsong, however muted, is sweeter in winter as it is so infrequent, except for the rather harsh note of the nuthatch, the chickadees' cheerful chatter, the cardinals' call, the screech of the blue jay, the rusty-gate remarks of the pheasant. None of this is song really; and it is sometimes accompanied by anxious twittering in the bare boughs of trees and the bleak branches of the leafless shrubs.

Here is true courage. With snow on the ground, ice in the driveway, and a wind cutting like a knife, or screaming about the eaves, with the threat of storm just around the corner, birds make themselves known to us.

In June the birds are certain of food and water; they find temporary apartments or build themselves homes; they have eggs to lay and babies to raise. They know that, barring accidents—cats or catastrophes—they have the whole wonderful summer before them. In winter it's a different story. They must—unless they go south—find shelter from gale and snow; they must hunt for and discover food; huddle in the woods, and survive as best they can. Sometimes mourning doves stay with me all winter; they aren't supposed to, you know. And always they'll sing in their winter way. In winter I don't even mind greedy, unclean, and voracious starlings for they too have a clear, high note.

Always, in the deadly chill or raging noises of winter—last winter was cold and stormy and the one before it, lethal—I listen for the small, brave sounds from fragile feathered throats and even if the snow lies two feet deep and the drifts pile up like ocean waves and the ice is a glistening treachery, whether the wind blows or not, I am comforted by the gallant speech of birds. This sound is as heartening as the flash of scarlet wings over the snow or the lovely blue of the jay teetering from a branch.

Courage is where you find it and has nothing to do with climate. And beyond courage there is hope, optimism, and the certain knowledge that one day it will be spring, and then, summer.

June being a romantic, is the most lighthearted and sentimental of months. I've often thought that St. Valentine's Day should fall in June when we have birds and graduates, the leafed-out trees, the beginning roses and the sheen of sunlight on blue water; in early June we have true spring and later, by the calendar, the start of summer. But in the valiance of a little bird in winter we have the promise of June long before it appears.

Usually in this enchanting month, one thinks of brides and, of course, roses, but my preoccupation this year is with daisies. I'm one of the few people who do not resent but rather enjoy dandelions, even in lawns, for they are small yellow suns. I recall how my father used to fight dandelions with executive strategy when we were on Shelter Island. He would gather together his family, all house guests, and any droppers-in, feed them lavishly, permit them a short rest after repletion, and then send them forth with trowels to uproot dandelions from the grass, while from the front porch he watched with benevolence this involuntary activity.

But no one can object to daisies, wherever they may grow. I look for them in my own fields, or someone else's, along all roadsides and beside railway tracks. They remind me of the time when, as a small girl, I was in upstate New York with my sister, her nurse, our grandmother, and an old friend of the family whom I called Aunt Molly. We were there because our mother, back in the city, was very ill with typhoid and it was considered expedient to remove the old and the young from her vicinity.

It must have been in June, for there was a graduation at the local school and I went with numerous children with whom I attended Sunday school to pick daisies and weave them into white, green, and golden chains to decorate the auditorium.

That's about all I do recall of that time except the big old house where we were lodged and the dam which blew up within our sight and hearing. Or, was it a dam? I don't know. It was something anyway, which expressed itself in sound and fury and caused Aunt Molly to come flying down the stairs and out to the front porch, her bright blue hair streaming out behind her like an indigo banner. Her hair was, of course, white and she used a bluing, even way back then. I assume she hadn't had time to rinse most of the bluing out when the dam or whatever it was blew up. Oh, yes, one other thing: Aunt Molly tried to teach me to embroider—a lost cause, I must say—for she thought that my mother upon her recovery would be ecstatic at receiving a bureau scarf ornamented by my stubby and, I may add, grubby little hands. The embroidery, by the way, was a representation of daisies. I don't remember what my mother said when finally she saw it; I hope she didn't have a relapse.

Two other times in my life I made something for her which wasn't set down in words: I once took painting lessons, my first year in boarding school. I was, I think, about eleven. My only achievement was a small oil of stiff pansies in a sort of vase. I gave it to her; it vanished. Small wonder! And then, when I was in Germany, I learned to do very minute cross stitching. I managed to produce a little house, a walk, and a border of flowers. It ruined my eyes and my temper but she had it framed, on my return home and probably hid it shortly thereafter. I think one of my children has it now (undoubtedly also hidden).

Looking back, I recall that my father took us upstate that distant June. I remember nothing of the train trip but a little of the drive to the lake near which the lodginghouse was situated, for we were driven in a species of buckboard over what is known as corduroy road. I fancy that Aunt Molly was vocal about it, that my sister slept, and I just looked; and I am certain that our remarkable grandmother was patient; she always was, all the years I knew her, and she came to live with the Baldwins when her daughter (my mother) was married. She died in her eighties while I was in Germany.

Funny thing about that lake, I can't find it on the map. I know it was in or near the town of Liberty, but many years later when I lived in a Connecticut town, just a hoot and a holler from this one, I came to know the manager of the motion-picture theater there and he turned out to be related to the ladies who owned and operated that lakeside lodginghouse in which we lived briefly that faraway June.

Daisies have been on my mind since Christmas, for around the holidays I had a letter from an Englishman whom I have known since he stayed with us, for a long weekend, in the other house. It was during the Second World War and he, together with a lad from South Africa and one from Australia, had been in Canada. They were the RAF . . . and, if my memory serves me, they came to the United States to pick up some planes—if ever you pick planes up—and fly them, I suppose, to Canada. I never saw my South African or my Australian again, though the former wrote me for a time and when I was in Australia, in 1954, the mother of my Australian telephoned me. But the Englishman, whose given name is Kenneth, has written to me every year and sent me little drawings. I remember how, when he was with us, he'd sit in the garden and draw. He was very young of course; and wanted to be an architect; he was already married when first I knew him.

I didn't see him again until 1954 when I was in London and he and his wife drove a long distance to spend a day with me. I remember we never left my rooms in the London hotel—we just talked and ate; lunch, tea, supper.

Later Kenneth came to this country with a friend on a business trip and they stayed with me for a short weekend. It rained most of the time, but they were bird watchers and didn't mind; they knew that some birds venture out, and sing, in the rain. The first morning they were here I looked from my windows and saw what I'd never seen before, a rose-breasted grosbeak in the feeder. I ran to thunder on the door of the double guest room. No answer. When later, dressed and in my right mind, I went down to breakfast, there they were. They had a camera set up in the big south window and had seen the grosbeak before I did.

It was of his trips here that Kenneth wrote me, this past Christmas. He spoke of the various disappointments encountered during his two visits to the States and also of the things which had interested and pleased him. He said that he'd discovered that he was more excited by detail than by the over-all picture.

"For me," he wrote, "the details make the whole and a grand

91

effect is not sufficient. There's more in the heart of a daisy than in the whole field."

I've often thought of that since. You know how we say we "can't see the forest for the trees"? Perhaps it sometimes works the other way around; we cannot, often, see the one great towering tree for the forest.

Let's put it another way. When we look at a great painting, we rarely study the detail; simply, the entire work of art itself, the stunning, breath-taking effect. But since Kenneth's letter I've been looking for detail in many things. For instance, a painting which is all colors, seeming movement and crowds, such as the Dutch, Flemish, and Italian masters painted for all time. You look at such a painting and forget the small details which compose it; look closer and you will see a child playing alone; a woman with a serene face; an old, grave man with all the beauty of character and long living drawn or painted there. A hundred, a thousand such details make up the whole. In the scenes of sorrow and suffering, in the scenes of torture and war, in the depiction of streets and interiors there are details of hope and courage and beauty which we overlook in the impact of the whole. Look again, and we can see a tiny cherub face at the edge of a dark cloud; or a flash of sun in the far corner.

Most of us, looking back upon our lives, see them more or less whole, or if we do remember detail it is not the golden heart of the daisy but the canker in the equally golden heart of the rose. We remember the disaster, the overwhelming grief or disappointment; we recall the painful wrench of loss and struggle and forget the other details which are as the daisy's heart. We forget the friends who came to our rescue, the unspectacular steady love we've been given, the understanding we've received lifelong, and the happiness and strength bestowed upon us.

God operates in the over-all picture but also in the smallest, blessed detail; the light shining through darkness, the quiet word spoken at the right time, the touch of a hand, light and consoling.

In this month I hope to be with my sister again. Long before I arrive she has projects on the fire of her enthusiasms cooking for me. She's a great one for projects and she inherited our father's fancy for the trowel in other people's hands, although, I must say, that she works right along with me, and anyone else, which he did not.

So if all goes well, I'll be with her once more by the sea and we will look again upon the ancient, very cold ocean and on warm days, perhaps, take a picnic lunch to the shelter of the dunes. We'll go shopping, attend meetings, and have dinner out now and again. If it's warm, we'll sit on the terrace for breakfast, have tea on the lawn and sun bathe when the sun is out. It doesn't matter what we do or what projects she has in mind, as long as we are together. She'll cook, and I'll set the table, dropping things as usual, and we'll talk of the days gone by. Last year she told me about Greece and this year she'll bring me up to date on Egypt. We'll talk about her children and mine and the days will drift past, the lazy June days, sometimes bright with sun and sometimes singing with rain.

It's strange, but nothing seems very threatening in June, not even sudden cold or thunder storms. It's June, we say to one another, and so nothing unpleasant can last very long.

If I do as I've done several times I'll take a small plane home which will fly low over the water, and I'll look down and see the white wakes of little boats upon the blue.

There will be daisies in my sister's meadows as well as here at home. I'll look for them upspringing on delicate stems—yet sturdy, too. Have you ever tried to pick them? With their faces turned upward, they are like white stars in the grass. And they grow in places where it's amazing to find anything rooted, and never, I think, alone. A daisy seems always to have a companion, one, or many. And while I shall admire the field or the meadow or the daisies blooming along a road side, I'll stoop to one flower only and look into the golden little heart.

I have often written and spoken of my mother's passion for flowers. At Hilo Farm she had big, lovely, informal gardens and people to cut the flowers and bring them to the house in flat baskets to be arranged. But often she'd send me into the fields to pick the wild blossoms—butter and eggs, Queen Ann's lace, wild roses, and sprays of berry blossoms—though most wild flowers have short lives, once cut. I rather resented these excursions for, like all young people, I had what appeared to me more attractive, immediate things to do than run parental errands. Now, in retrospect, I wonder if my mother was not sometimes a little weary of the cultivated order of her gardens and the baskets brimming with bloom. Perhaps she wanted to be surrounded, however briefly, with wild free-growing, humble beauty, which, untended, often unnoticed, lives and dies as a part of the landscape; a detail of the whole. Perhaps she, too, wanted to look into the heart of a daisy.

Now, in this month, I think of all the young people who set their feet upon another path; for as has been said "the longest journey begins with the first step." There are those who approach an altar and those who will graduate from schools or colleges begin the search for work and self-justification.

In June the world should be at peace, as nature is. To be at peace never means idleness. The trees strain, and burst with green energy, the roses put forth their best, most scented effort, and the new Spartans, a Christmas present that came to me at planting time, now they fashion little leaves and endeavor to achieve first bloom.

When things go wrong on this Little Earth, I try to remember the timid but insistent sound of bird cries in the winter and to realize that there is no time when we do not find challenge and none when there's no need for courage, hope, and trust.

The bird has faith in spring; he has this faith even through the bleak and bitter months. For no matter what happens, nature continues to roll the seasons' hoop and June comes, always.

So we too can trust, whatever may be the climate of the tired heart.

All difficulties are details of the big picture which is living, and there is song on the coldest day and back of the darkened sky, steadfast light.

As one grows older in years, the seasons seem to roll more swiftly;

94

hardly has the Christmas tree been taken out, the glitter gone, denuded of all ornamentation, before we are watching the snow melt and anticipating Easter, and then June.

In the equable seasons of the human spirit I like to think—no matter what the mind, or heart, or calendar says—it is forever June.

<img centered decorative ornament />

"A house with lawns enclosing it . . ."
ROBERT LOUIS STEVENSON

This quotation is not really applicable. There's very little grass on the west and north sides of the house; east and south are better, but as this property is built, lawns and all upon sand and gravel, what grass there is is very patchy indeed. Where the big trees grow there's mostly moss, and the slopes down to the pond or up to the bird bath abound in weeds and crab grass; in dry seasons—and most midsummers are dry—the brightest green spot is around the bird bath because we so often fill it, and also the birds happily splash the water out of the millstone which is their property.

The single guest room looks west and north. This is a catch-all room. It wasn't, at one time, but it is now. It's rarely used as a guest room, and I've loaded the clothes closet and bureau drawers, for in this room I pack. It's wonderful to have a place in which to pack and unpack. Here are the summer frocks which I didn't banish to the attic, and a sort of tossed salad of summer shoes, and in the bureau all sorts of things that I use only when I go away.

There's a bookcase there with not much in it except a few old books and some of the mugs I spoke of earlier; there's a chair or two, a low table, and a bed which belonged to my mother. I always thought of it as a swan bed, but an antique-dealer friend tells me it's gooseneck. Well, if ducklings can become swans, why can't geese?

It's a nice bed. I lie on it sometimes when the sunroom is too dazzling or too hot, or because my own bed is too near a telephone.

95

Someone asked me recently if, in this house, I had a prayer room, and the answer was no. I have friends who have set aside quiet corners, not necessarily whole rooms, where they can sit to meditate and pray. This is a wonderful and helpful practice, but mine is a house of interruptions: people, doorbells, telephones, to say nothing of deadlines and the can't-be-put-aside work. The one time I'm pretty sure of no interruptions is in the very early morning and then I find my own bedroom a perfectly fine place for giving thanks and asking guidance. Evenings before I go to bed, I'm not so sure; people are apt to call me any time, but after midnight, unless there is a catastrophe or a wrong number, I can usually be still out in the sunroom which, by then, is filled with stars.

But any place can be a prayer room: whether you're washing dishes or walking down a road, whether you're in a plane or bus or train; whether you're sewing or using a broom. For often the desire for communication with God is so intense that there need be no words, simply a voiceless cry of thanksgiving, or for help or understanding. Without the help I've had, without faith which once I lost and then recovered, I would not now be alive in this world.

I believe all prayers are answered; not perhaps as we wish them to be, but in God's way and will, which isn't usually ours. All God's ways are mysterious, but His spiritual laws are simple and plain: Order, Law, Balance and always the Golden Rule. The selfless prayer reaches its goal and I know that my prayers for others have often been answered. This is a type of sharing; and to receive one must give.

Prayer is trust and faith in operation; answered prayer is love in operation. All prayer is good, and serves a powerful purpose: the prayer in church which unite with those of others; the ritual, the formal prayer, the talking aloud to the inner self, which is part of the Divine; the silent call, the prayer at one's desk or out of doors, while watching a sunset, or a storm, or the flow of quiet or raging waters; and the prayers in the dark nights or lonely dawns.

The spirits of men struggle to manifest through the erring, stubborn density of the flesh and of the physical mind; almost always the link between is corroded. Prayer is the higher self endeavoring to speak; it is reaching for a hand; it is often spontaneous and unselfish petition; prayer, in secret, remains a secret.

The single guest room would, I think, make a prayer room. Even as it now is, cluttered but not near a telephone, it is a good place in which to rest for a little while, half awake, half asleep, and send the kite of prayer soaring on the high wind of the spirit.

From the west windows of this room, as from those in my bedroom and study, I can see the sunset, and from here I often take the time to really see it, not just to glance and look away. In the study, if I am working, I'm not apt to look for long, for except in the long summer days the lights must go on if I'm to work. In my bedroom I glance up from the dressing table, but in the single guest room, I lie on the gooseneck bed and watch, through two windows, the ineffable glory of the heavens.

And sometimes I wonder who lived in this room, for what purpose it was used a hundred years ago, or more. How many people before me have rested here, wept, laughed, or prayed? How many watched the sunset?

I'll never know that, but this I do know: that in the quiet moments, the periods of reflection, we are never alone; we are always companioned.

Despite our continual tensions and anxieties and the fears which sometimes crash over our heads like enormous waves to send us choking, blind and struggling, to the bottom for a time, there's nothing of which to be afraid. For sooner or later, according to the lifeline of our belief, we come to the sunlit surface and to quiet water.

July

Whatever happened to what Samuel Taylor Coleridge called "the leafy month of June"? I haven't the least idea and, for that matter, whatever happened to the mint which for some years grew by the kitchen door? I can't find that, either.

Lately I've been thinking of the seasons, not only as a hoop but as a landscape, always altering. Winter is a long, difficult, and slippery hill, but on the way up the scene changes, the blue deepens in the sky, the snow and ice melt and there's spring. Perhaps June is an easier way to another hilltop, crested and foamed with blossom. Then comes the easy, downward slope; you slide into July, at the bottom of the hill, into the tall grass and the trees crowded with foliage, and into showers of bloom in the gardens and a sunburst of fireworks . . . but silent ones. I hate noise. I don't mind the kind of fireworks that go off with an apologetic little bang and burst into fountains of stars against a summer sky. I like those, really.

I hadn't seen a big display for many years until last July when I was with friends at a country club in Westchester. It was fun to sit at a terrace table and watch rockets and comets—professionally set off, so I knew no one would be hurt.

I wonder what happened to the set pieces of my youth? Seems

to me that I remember one that was called The Fall of Port Arthur.

July is also a kind of circus with at least six rings—vacations—and a big top, which is all the sky; and the clowns of laughter.

When I spent summers on Shelter Island, the circus under a canvas top came annually to Greenport, so we used to take the old ferry and chug across bright water. It was a traveling circus, and small; the seats were continuous benches and uncomfortable, and I was always afraid of falling down between the rows. I recall vividly the time I entered the tent and was closely followed by a real clown who mimicked my walk and gestures. I was terribly embarrassed and, anyway, as long as I can remember, I've felt uneasy about circus clowns. Even the least talented always seemed to me on the verge of tragedy, as if they teetered over a cliff on a high wire. They were for crying over, rather than laughing at, I thought.

In later years I took my children to the big circus which comes to New York in the spring and is housed in Madison Square Garden. Having a horror of heights—except in airplanes where the vision is wide and practically unrestricted—I always closed my eyes when the acrobats walked the wire or swung from trapezes. I remember once putting out my hand and having it firmly grasped. I didn't know until I dared to open my eyes again that a child sitting in the next box against the partition, as I was sitting in ours, had also reached for the nearest support, which happened to be me.

Often I've regretted that my children never saw that little tent circus in the country. You could see at once everything that was going on; there was just one ring. In the big circus what ring do you watch? You can't watch them all.

Life is, I daresay, very like a many-ringed circus and no one operates on just one level. All of us function in a number of rings; the physical and material; the spiritual, the mental, the emotional.

And there are challenges and dangers; high-diving acts of courage; the precarious balancing, the bids for attention, the clowning.

Often we ourselves are the clowns, with laughter which breaks upon tears and what we sometimes believe to be tragedy, which is

99

closer to ironic comedy. Yes, I think we are the clowns . . . and also the acrobats, the wire walkers, and the ringmasters cracking the whips.

It is interesting to ponder that as we lead our frenetic, helter-skelter lives on the physical plane of existence, we are, at the same time, leading the mental lives of our thoughts, wondering and sometimes confused; and, even stranger, that beyond the functioning of the inquiring mind, the last and most important ring level remains—that of quiet spiritual acceptance or rejection.

All rings are linked, one with the other, and sometimes they are most difficult to separate; in fact, perhaps they cannot really be separated at all.

Present-day living is very bewildering, but hasn't it always been so? Every era has brought tension, threat, and difficulties to those who have lived in it.

Now there are simply more potent threats and a great many more people to be aware of them—and of one another. A generation or so ago we were blandly unaware of anything which happened in, say Africa: excepting, possibly, the Boer War. Now we have lost our ignorance, for modern methods of communication bring us close to every place on this planet and to all people.

I suppose that the best we can do in this multiple-ringed circus we call life is to live as fully and wisely as possible amid the uproar, to retreat as often as we can from the lunatic pace of our physical, mental, and emotional preoccupations into the most important ring of all, which is probably unnoticed by any spectator who observes our outward antics, but is the spiritual center of all life, the center within ourselves, in which any activity, however unseen, is of utmost importance.

While we swing from the trapezes and bars, with or without nets beneath us; fly through the uncaring air, or totter along the taut-strung wires; while we ride bareback upon the horses of ambition and seek to tame the lions and tigers of fear and frustration; as we put on the make-up and assume the postures of a clown to fool ourselves and others, the spiritual life continues, quiet, inexorable, and enduring.

Through our physical life we learn, we are taught by failure and by success; through the mental life we widen our small understanding of ourselves, others, and the world in which we live; through the emotional life we are taught to suffer and to rejoice; all these lives are interlocked, but through the spiritual life, if we remember to live it, we grow.

This month, which has made me think of fireworks and circuses, is sleepy. I look back on June as a season of happy activity with my sister on Long Island, and July seems to me to be a drowsy interval between Long Island and Cape Cod. Most people think of it in terms of holidays, crowded roads, airplanes to heaven knows where, and ships which sail the seven seas. A good many people think of it as a month in which other people come to visit them or they go visiting . . . welcome often, and often, not. But I regard it as just drowsy. The heavy leaves on the trees are dimmed by dust; the trees themselves stand knee deep in tall grass and time, for me, moves slowly, more like an idle backwater rather than a rushing stream.

I'll be working all month at this or that unless it is made possible for me to go winging across country to Colorado for a brief visit with my younger daughter ("Bon Flyage" as a dear friend of mine remarks when someone is flying rather than sailing away). But if and when I'm home, I'll take time out to sit on my small terrace, provided the mosquitoes have decided to go elsewhere (and happy flyage to them, too), or put the rattan shades down in the sunroom, stay there for a while, and take time out to think about people and places.

It has for years astonished me how, despite their outward differences, people are basically so much alike. Last winter the pastor of my church, speaking of the various religions followed and practiced by the peoples of the world, remarked that it is a pity how much we dwell upon the differences, whereas it would be so much better to consider the similarities. Take, for instance, the Golden Rule; in one form or another it is to be found in all religions, even before Christianity.

We are very apt to ponder the differences in races, nationalities, and individuals, usually considering them from our own backgrounds of race, and nationality, and from our own viewpoints as individuals. Yet everyone has something in common with everyone else. Essentially it is mortality and immortality; and it is, or should be, the consciousness of the divine spark in all of us, the human spirit, which is the common denominator, the ability to feel pain, to suffer or rejoice. All people are born; all at some time grieve, and at some time are happy; all look forward with hope, and backward with regret; all hunger and thirst; all work and play; and in the body all eventually die.

Yet there are more similarities than these, if less important. How often have we met people with whom we feel we have nothing in common aside from the indisputable fact that we are human beings. But haven't we? I think there are very few people, perhaps none, from whom we cannot learn something, and certainly none who haven't—if we look closely and deeply enough—some resemblance to ourselves.

We may differ widely in background, education, learning, and knowledge—or the lack of them—and in personalities, likes, and dislikes. But if we try, we can find a meeting ground somehow, somewhere. It may be a shared rooted belief; it may be something as trivial as a fancy for the color pink or for chocolate cake; it can be a love of flowers, an interest in any of the arts or professions, a passion for cooking or for antique hunting. Perhaps it's skin diving or skiing, beach walks or reading; perhaps the same kind of humor amuses us. . . . In what we may at first believe to be the person most unlikely to resemble ourselves at all, we can find similarity. I have, often enough. Sometimes we don't like certain people because much of the fault we find with others is the reflection of our own unacknowledged faults, but there's a meeting ground, too—the faults. Anyway if we search for it, we can be unwillingly or happily amazed to find that we stand together on shared ground.

Well, anyway most of us do agree about weather although I have one friend who swears that it can never become hot enough

102

for her; now that I come to think of it, I have two such extraordinary friends.

I have often said or written that each person is unique and that all people differ, one from the other, as snowflakes do, but even snowflakes, millions upon millions, of them, each infinitesimally differing from the next, have in common the substance which shapes them.

Once we discover that each person we meet is an individual in his own right and never a carbon copy of anyone else, yet that each in some fashion is akin to us, we'll find that there's no one in this world with whom we cannot communicate. Strange languages are certainly barriers, but there are other means of communication. We can sense this if we are listening to the same music or looking at the same landscape or painting; and a smile is universal, it needs no translation. I have knelt in churches where no word of English was spoken, but I could still worship with those around me; and from whatever environment or walk of life a person comes, he or she has something to contribute to our own store of knowledge and somewhere along the line we will find ourselves in agreement.

There will be disagreement also, of course, but I'm growing a little tired of people who dismiss others as stupid simply because they don't agree with them! I believe, with my pastor, that the emphasis should be on the similarities. Men—and some women, too—often make fun of the women who meet and in no time at all are talking about their children, their domestic and shopping problems, and what goes on in the kitchen, laundry, or playground. Actually, half a dozen women can be as different one from the other as baked beans from caviar but in voicing what to the cynical listener appears to be commonplace trivia, they have found a meeting ground. Once that most astute observer of life, the New York City taxi driver, finds out I'm interested in baseball, politics, and what makes people tick, we become garrulous friends. Maybe his team isn't my team nor his party my party, but he likes people, too, and he knows that with friendly passengers agreement can be reached, or a valid discussion started—and a discussion isn't an argument.

That is the way we learn from others, not only from our own close-knit circle of relatives and friends but from chance-met strangers, the person to whom we are introduced at a party, or who sits beside us in plane, bus, or train; someone we speak to on the deck of a ship, or in a resort; the one we find near us at some public function, or encounter going up the steps of a church or into a lecture hall. These are people we may never see again, but to listen is to learn.

It is generally accepted that we can learn from people older than ourselves if we are willing to suffer repetition, or leap the occasional hurdle of boredom or impatience. It is also accepted that we can learn from children; and here again patience is a factor. I have heard the most illuminating wisdom from little people not yet old enough to mask their natural candor.

But we can also learn from our contemporaries even if we don't happen to like them all. I sometimes think you can learn as much from people you do not like as from those you do. Perhaps even more!

Tonight when I go up to the sunroom, after a little walk in the cooling darkness, I'll look from the south windows at the starry sky. Stars seen through the unassisted human eye seem very much alike; they aren't, of course, though they have similarities, beginning with the basic one of shedding light, of luminous shining in the dark.

There are people like stars who, without a word and often quite unconsciously, illuminate our path with a steady shining in the dark. There are people whose courage is a quiet light upon their own paths.

Recently I had occasion to talk for quite a long time to a woman I met here in my own house one evening. She had come on an unimportant errand and stayed to visit awhile. The few times I'd seen her she'd seemed to me to be a gay, sincere little person, ready with laughter and sympathy. Through our conversation I learned that for a long while hers had been a very rough path, indeed, and still was. She had, when she talked to me, a serious and immediate problem. She thought she'd found the solution. I thought so, too, but the next time I saw her it appeared it was not the solution after all, but that, if the problem were to be solved, she would have to take the one step she dreaded above everything else. I have no doubt she'll take it, and that when, after that step, the door she's been trying to keep open closes, there will be another door, and the key to that is in her own hand, for it is courage.

Last winter I spoke at an interracial meeting at a church. It wasn't the first such meeting at which I'd spoken, nor will it be the last. Afterward we all had a wonderfully good buffet supper together and talked among ourselves. I learned a great deal that evening, and all of it was good, and I'll take time to think about it this month, as I have every month since . . . and of the Intelligence which shaped us all and made us, whatever our differences, kinsfolk.

I just stopped to look at a calendar. Incredible as it may seem we have had only one Friday the thirteenth this year and that was in March; I was walking on a beach that day. The next one comes in November. "Now why," asked someone walking into the study and seeing me looking at the calendar, "are you interested?"

Because I like Friday the thirteenth, that's why; and my father did before me. I remember when, turned twenty-one or so, I had elective surgery and could select my own day. I chose Friday the thirteenth and also asked for a young, pretty, and if possible red-headed nurse.

Perhaps my father and I were superstitious in reverse; I've always liked Fridays and I love the thirteenth. Perhaps, in openly denying the superstition, we thought, father and I, that we'd be rewarded. Perhaps it is because astrology informs me that Friday is my lucky day, though I'm afraid that's not so. I've been just as lucky on Thursday, for instance, or as unlucky.

Butterfly weed will still be growing in my fields this month. And on the fourth, if I am here and alone, I can see from upstairs the fireworks set off in the distance at a golf or beach club. All I will see, of course, will be a lazy cascade of stars falling. Many of my friends will be away on holiday or if the month is as hot as usual, just sitting, screaming silently in air-conditioned rooms. August's hot, too, but usually relents at night. And lazy as I am and as I believe July to be, I'll work because there is no better way than work to forget anything whether it be worry, grief, or heat for a little while. Last year in midsummer I was having a dreadful time trying to write a novel, so I found all sorts of wild excuses not to work. I would have been a lot better off if I'd just worked and then torn up the pages at day's end. I wouldn't have thought about how hot it was!

Now time stands still a little and the birds go deep into the woods. People who are off and about the pleasant business of vacationing—often doing so much in a short time that they really need a holiday thereafter—won't think so, but July is like a slow-drawn breath held for a moment between quick, hurrying breaths. And if we pause to pray, to think and wonder, we shall have found for an instant of time the quiet, drowsy backwater which strengthens, refreshes, and sustains.

❦ ❧

"Set thine house in order . . ."
ISAIAH 38:1

When it comes to the back rooms—there are two of these and a shower room—you reach them through the big bathroom or by going up the back stairs from the kitchen.

After we moved we didn't do much about this little separate apartment, but when my older daughter and her children live here for some months, they were put there, with cribs and the necessities; not enough room for them really, but the front part of the house was dangerous, even with a gate up, because the stairs are open at the top; on back stairs, you can close a door. When my younger son came home, he had what he needed there and could come and go unbeknownst to me.

Eventually, realizing that the time might come when I'd need someone here at night, I turned these back rooms into a little suite—a small living room, with big couch, side table (a record holder really), chair, and chest of drawers; and back of that the single bedroom, also with a record holder for a night table, a book-case, dressing table, and chair. We bought unpainted furniture and had that painted, redid the floors and found rugs and also reproduction lamps. It's quite pretty really and anyone living back there can close two doors between herself and the hall.

The finished apartment hasn't been used much: once for a dear friend who feared her coughing would disturb others, and during the time my young Australian nurse was here; she loves privacy, which she had seldom had to any extent, and she loved having her own shower and own place to lie down and read and nap. At any rate, the apartment is there for the guest who may prefer it, or for any emergency. It's a quiet suite, with two west windows and an east in the living room, and two west, two small north and an east in the bedroom. To be sure the bedroom overlooks the drive-way, but that isn't exactly teeming with cars at any time.

My possessions overflow into the little apartment, too; I leave things on the bed after ironing; there is a linen closet as well as a clothes closet where we hang things, and I admit to using some drawers of the high chest to put away Christmas mats and table-cloths!

Every time I go into my room, I am reminded of Isaiah saying, "Set your house in order." Actually his words referred to the illness of Hezekiah. Isaiah bade him set his house in order, for he was to die. But he did not; God answered Hezekiah's prayer and he re-covered. Well, thanks to Agnes' help, this house is in order, in spite of the hidden-away overflow. I am by nature orderly, a trait I inherited from my father, who used to stand on the veranda of the country house and point with rage to a scrap of paper blowing across the lawns or under the apple trees. He would shout for immediate service and bring people running from important work

107

in field or garden to pick up the dreadful object. I, too, have a slight attack of the screaming meemies when, during high winds, on the days the big back porch trash basket is emptied, some of the enormous amount of paper in it escapes and frolics all over, usually winding up in almost inaccessible places under trees and bushes. I go chasing them with the fervor usually characteristic of those who chase butterflies and rainbows. I feel this way about roadside litter, too, and am livid when, on occasion, I climb over the stone wall and into the corner property to look for flowers and find instead all sorts of unpleasant wreckage flung from passing cars!

But it is not just the material house which needs order. And to set one's mental, emotional, and spiritual house aright is no small task. I try, and sometimes, for a few hours, think that I've succeeded, but the next moment there it is all untidy again. In the attic of one's memory there are many useless things which we believe we have discarded for good, but which turn up again when we go poking in dusty corners. Just a yearly turnout isn't of much help; you overlook a good deal. I suppose it's better not to put anything in that attic which isn't joyous or helpful or—like a textbook—a lesson.

There are dark corners of the heart as well as of the mind that need to be cleansed of the painful and destructive emotions of which there are so many.

Spiritually, setting one's house in order is, I think, a matter of bringing in useful, nourishing qualities than of discarding anything; for the spiritual house is an expanding one; as we grow, it grows with us.

If only we could empty out, throw away, burn, or otherwise destroy all the accumulations of the years which are of no value and can be of considerable harm! But every day brings something we are inclined to keep, even if we shouldn't, so setting one's house in order is a daily, an hourly task.

Sunlight flooding a room which appears to be in perfect order will, as you must have noticed, hunt out all the dust on the tables and shelves, dust you do not notice when the sun isn't betraying your housekeeping. So, too, spiritual sunlight, flooding mind and heart, will reveal the dust there in the clear light of honesty; and then we have to dust again.

Actually, and literally, I rather like to dust. I hate scrubbing sinks, and I loathe running a vacuum cleaner, but dusting I like. And, if I'm all alone in a quiet kitchen with lots of hot water and soap, I enjoy washing dishes. If there aren't too many, I find it soothing. . . .

And so, we set the house in order for August.

August

During this month, on my way down to the pond to see if my old Chinese frog still stands on the rim and if there's water for him to look into or just a muddy puddle, I usually deviate a little to look under the ancient apple trees for windfalls of August apples. These are never many nor much to look at, nor are they good to eat out of the hand, but they make fine apple sauce and I like to hear them falling into the grass at night when I'm in the sunroom with the windows open; the sound is as round as the apples should be.

The woodchucks like them. They sit up under the trees, eat the fruit out of their little black hands, and what they don't like they discard.

In this month, barring changes of plans, accidents, or unexpected turns in the road, I should be going back to the Cape where I shall breathe a different, headier air, see my friends, and take the Irish for a run on the beach (if the lady the Irish owns permits).

As always when I'm to go away, I start wondering what to pack, and what to leave at home. It has been my fate for many years that, wherever I'm going—south, east, west, around the world, or merely around the corner or across the street—to take what I won't need and to leave behind things which I'll discover, soon enough are vital to welfare or wardrobe. I seem to be destined to leave the belts of dresses at home.

I sometimes think that this is because I am too well organized. I start to pack weeks ahead; that is to say, I put things in the bureau or closet of the single guest room in readiness for packing, and then, of course, I need something before I depart so I hunt it up, use it, and forget to put it back again; often I mislay it entirely.

One thing I'm sure of, no matter what I bring, or do not bring, to Gladys Taber's house on the cove, is a welcome.

August makes me think of lighthouses which are found all over the world, wherever there's a coastline. I see them on Long Island in June; I've seen them in California; but my earliest memories stem from the Cape which I saw first when I was three years old.

I've always been drawn to this particular type of structure. I remember one which wasn't in the water but on a point of land by the St. Lawrence, and another on a hill in Nova Scotia, looking across a road and a great many rocks. I climbed that one: seven flights of steps, the last two being ladders.

Not all lighthouses live with their feet in the sea to be reached only by boat, and many, along the Atlantic coast at least, have been abandoned as other methods and measures for saving ships and lives have come into use.

Occasionally you read in a paper that there's a lighthouse for sale. I've always thought it would be extraordinarily romantic to buy and live in one. Imagine getting up in the morning, baiting a hook, and dropping it from a window into the ocean to lure an early swimming fish to the breakfast table!

Lighthouses symbolize many things to me: far-reaching, steady light of course, upon land and water; strength, solidity, and the facing of storm and wind, rain and snow without trembling or flinching.

I have a young friend who lives in Chicago who used to complain that when I went to the Cape I never sent him any picture postals except those depicting lighthouses. There were many to

111

choose from, he argued; there must be postcards of houses, beaches, fishermen, sunsets, lobster pots, dunes, and roses. Of course there were, but I didn't send them to him. He could hardly wait to get there himself one summer weekend when he was in New England so he could send me a lighthouse. Later, when he went to Paris, he apologized on a picture postal—I think it was of the Eiffel tower— because he hadn't been able to find one of a lighthouse.

Actually the lighthouse represents much that we need and greatly desire: stability, illumination, a bright path cutting across darkness and security in storm.

We often speak of the inner citadel which is in each of us, the fortress to which, once we have learned the way, we can withdraw in times of stress. I like to visualize this as a spiritual lighthouse; never as an ivory tower, for that is simply an escape from life. A lighthouse isn't an escape; it warns, it guides, it stands firm, and above all it is a repository of radiance which illuminates murky corners.

This is a structure we must build ourselves; no one can do it for us. I'm sure we are all born with the necessary basic materials with which to construct our lighthouses, but sometimes it takes us a long time—it took me a long time, at any rate—to search for and discover the substance upon which we can lay the foundations. The substance is Faith; the foundations, Trust.

Thereafter, one builds slowly, painfully and, sometimes not very well. The design goes wrong or we do not follow the plan which is accurate and so the first bad blow may topple our lighthouse from its foundations and then we have to start over again.

How often have I stood with my comrades, Gladys and Eleanor, near Nauset Light and watched, as Gladys always says, "the waves come in from Spain." In the daylight, under the dazzling sun, you do not expect to see the lighthouse light, but you know it's there and as soon as that part of the world darkens it will shine upon the sea, the ships which sail it, and the shore.

When all goes well with us, we feel no driving urge to look inward. Why should we? The sun's shining. Yet, we should, I think, if only in order to give thanks.

But when the gales scream and the storm rages and there is no discernible light in our personal sky, we are forced to look for it and for strength; and we can find it if we have built this inner security and know how to approach it. Then we can be certain of calm, new hope, and light; always light. Which is, I think, one of the loveliest words in our language.

In the symbol of the lighthouse standing firm and beneficently casting the radiance toward which we look for help there is also the symbol of God; an awareness of the ever-present help in time of trouble; the knowledge that there is guidance for the most confused and lost, for those who have strayed from their course into strange and dangerous waters; and always light upon the darkest sea.

There are people who are like lighthouses, who merely by being themselves can bring to others a sense of peace, quiet reassurance and guidance which need not be expressed in words. These are the people who have constructed slowly, often out of suffering, their own inner resources and who have learned to share them with others, for the light which is within them shines not only across their own paths but across those of everyone they meet.

Where I live there are no lighthouses very near. There is, however, a beacon which I can see at night from the sunroom. It is punctual as it sweeps across the horizon. I have never asked where it is, or what it's there for—perhaps to guide aircraft toward their landings? I know a pilot or two and someday I'll ask. For now I'm content to lie on the couch, look from the windows, and see this unfailing light flash, sweep on and flash again.

One of the pilots I know spoke to me some time ago of the lighted steeples of churches of which there are several in our vicinity. He spoke of one in particular, tall, white, up-reaching and with a light on it. He said, "I always look for it."

He had all the instruments made available to him by science and he knew the way to his field, just as he knew his way to his own home, by car, train, or on foot, but still he looked for the special light.

We all do. We look for it in many places as well as within ourselves, for it is necessary to us. It is also what the world most needs and has always needed—light—whether from lighthouse, beacon, blazing sun, moon or star, or from a church spire reflecting the light cast upon it. Light on dark waters, in a nighttime sky, or upon the shadowed land, showing the way. These are symbols. Light is in itself a symbol. Peace is light, and love is light, and God is light—forever.

Almost everyone I know is trying desperately to get somewhere and every so often they find themselves blocked. It's easy to name the road barriers: fear, frustration, anger, circumstances, despair, or sudden darkness through which they cannot find a way back to their roads.

Most of us build the barriers over which we stumble. Not many months ago, when I crashed through a road block which was entirely of my own making, I realized that whatever came of this bruising break-through, I had succeeded in the vital venture, which is the effort.

There are so many things we deeply desire to achieve—material success in all fields of endeavor, peace of mind, security in its several forms, and inner quiet; and there are many things we equally desire for those we love. Most of us want more than one thing and set these as goals. Few of us succeed as we'd wish; some not at all.

But the real achievement is in the breaking down—and through— whatever blocks we have set up, or which circumstances have fashioned; achievement is the overcoming of obstacles, the taking of hurdles, and the impetus which sends us forward. It is always the effort which counts, no matter what does or does not come of it.

Living is a continually creative process, and we are all creative, each in our several ways. Creativity is not confined to the various fields of the arts. It flourishes in the kitchen, the garden, and the living room. It is in the factory and workshop and in the business office. It is in every branch of science and all the professions. It is in keeping a house and raising children. Creativity is planning, doing, and being; it is in making the effort, it is in the realization that you *are* creative, no matter what you do, as long as you go forward in usefulness and in self-expression.

Creativity is also—and profoundly—our attitude toward others. We make all our human relationships come alive through it; it is at the roots of every family and present in every human contact, however brief, or casual. No one is just part of an audience, just a reader, a housewife, a teacher, or parent. No one is "just" anything. Everyone is himself. There's none identical with him, although, as I said earlier, each man has something in common with every other. Everyone possesses, after his own fashion, the gift of creativity and the power to make a great contribution to his family, his friends, and hence, to his community and to the world in which he lives.

The idlest conversation with friend or a stranger can start a chain reaction of thought, and thought translates itself into action for good or evil. Thought itself, even when unspoken, is creative and no one knows how far-reaching is its influence.

We can sometimes hazard a guess. I remember sitting with a friend and asking, "What's the matter?"

She said, "Oh, nothing that I can talk about" (and she didn't), "I'm just thinking dark thoughts."

I could feel them. I did not know what they were or anything of her situation, but the dark thoughts were there, all around me.

Sometimes I contemplate with astonishment my own unconsidered words or careless actions and am stunned when I think what havoc I may unwittingly have caused.

In a world in which it would appear that only the loudest voices are heard, the greatest talents recognized, and only the most publicized are applauded or condemned, few of us stop to remember that the small voice is also heard by someone, the quiet talent rewarded, and the least act of importance to someone.

The person you hurt without meaning to will remember and he may pass that wound on to someone else. The person you help without thinking much about it, if at all, may pass that on also.

The chain reaction.

Today we may say something which affords a little comfort or extend a hand which helps to lift someone over a difficult spot in the road; yet on this same day we may say the unkind word or refuse to hold out the hand. Each action, or lack of it, goes on indefinitely—I sometimes think into infinity—rather like the stone tossed into the water and the widening, overlapping circles thereafter; perhaps the very depths, which we cannot see, are stirred and alteration therefore takes place.

When we manage to break down barriers of our own making, we affect other people if only by example. Crashing through a road block does not always precede success as we gauge it. We may, and often do, fail to find the goal on the other side; we may not reach what we thought was our destination. But that's not the important thing; the endeavor is. Failure is not lack of success; failure is the unwillingness to risk failure.

I suppose, when walking a pleasant, sunny, and even an idle way, if we suddenly come upon a barrier, we are apt to try to walk around it, or to turn back and look for an easier path. But if we break through, daring to fail, the effort is worth anything which may—or may not—come of it. Effort—the forward direction—is like breathing; if you stop, you aren't alive.

There are so many things we take for granted such as the air and the water we drink. Until we are deprived of them, we do not think about them. It is so in the everyday ways of living, too. When, as occasionally happens, my furnace turns sulky and refuses to function, usually over a weekend or in zero weather, I become vividly aware of that square, squat creature which is usually purring like a mammoth cat in the cellar. And when the power fails for one or another reason, and I put my hand to a switch and there's no light, then I become conscious of the efforts of a great many people who work, by day and night, to enable that switch to respond to me.

Actually we can take nothing in this world for granted; science has not yet invented the perfect machine which will never go out of order or break down. We take for granted the roof above our heads and the food upon our tables and the beds in which we sleep. All this, too, can be taken from us. We take for granted our parents, children, friends, and all whom we most love. But they, too, can vanish from our physical sight through the processes of nature, or they may remove themselves from us by their own wish, or be gone from our thresholds because their way in the world takes them great distances.

It is only when they are separated from us by the inexorable law that every man has his life span here; or by their own desire because we have disagreed or quarreled, or because their roads lead to places thousands of miles from where we are, that we remember we should not have taken them for granted. Love should never be taken for granted.

I sometimes think we take kindness too much for granted. For instance, one sunny cold day last winter while I sat working, my friend Agnes asked me if she could do me a favor. She'd given me my noontime tray and usually departs directly thereafter. I said, "Of course," and she asked, "May I stay with you until Gussie comes?"

She knew that I was literally sweating the day out, for my younger daughter, who lives in Colorado, was undergoing surgery of a serious nature, and not for the first time. There were reasons why it was not expedient for me to be there during this operation and all I could do was wait to hear, and hold myself in readiness in case things were not as we anticipated and I'd be told to come.

I said, "I'm working. I'll be all right. You must have things to do at home."

She said she had not. She added, "Please?"

So she stayed, upstairs, and I went on working and when the first telephone call came that all was well so far, she went home, after asking me to stop working and try to rest.

You can't take that kind of offered hand for granted.

Nor could I take for granted my friends who said, "We'll come to dinner with you the night of the operation," and those who said, "We'll be over the night after."

When I was young I took everything for granted—a child does, of course—support, necessities, love, and security. But sometimes a child, young as he is, finds that these do not go on forever; many things can happen to disrupt his home and threaten his security. But I grew up taking everything as my due. I got over that quite a while ago. I know now that a door which has always

117

opened on warmth can suddenly open on cold and darkness and emptiness. I know that the source of heat can fail, as my furnace once did on the day of my child's operation. So I walk delicately, trying not to take all the good for granted, but to treasure it, to appreciate it, and to give thanks.

We mustn't take the bad for granted, either.

It is hard to walk the middle line between the unrealistic approach we call "Pollyanna" and the negative attitude. It is hard to think positively and at the same time to see clearly. But it can be done. I know many people who have achieved this balance. I do not count myself among their numbers, for I am often far too much like a pendulum, swinging from one side to the other. . . .

Now we swing into September, that lovely month which can behave like early spring, blow hot or cold, yet brings a special benediction.

❧ ☙

"Yea, the sparrow hath found an house"
PSALMS: 84: 3

We have about reached the end of the guided tour . . . unless anyone wants to sit on the front stairs with me, or climb the pull-down ladder to the attic, or descend into the cellar. But there are places out of doors which relate to the house and are, in a way, an extension of it.

The back porch has a roof, and that has a ledge, and within its shelter birds built their nests . . . probably sparrows. This ledge we finally blocked up because there was a little too much avian activity, so you hardly dared venture onto the porch what with the flying, and complaining, and downright hostile goings-on. But there are plenty of bushes growing round the porch and a big sheltering forsythia and it's a pleasant place to sit if you are so minded, despite the presence of the huge wastepaper basket. I always have

118

a couple of chairs out there in the summer. The view isn't exciting: small trees, big shrubs, and beyond them bigger trees and shrubs; the red-brick path, the driveway, the little red garage and a stone wall and back of it my good neighbors' towering pines.

You can get from the kitchen porch to the terrace if you step over a small space occupied only by air and land safely on the flagstones near the porch. There are chairs and little tables there once it grows warm and until it's cold again and from there you can see down the slope to the pines, dogwoods, apple trees, and the pond. When I was more energetic than now and I'd take a tray out there early in the morning and have breakfast. It had to be early, for after the sun was high it was too hot to sit there until afternoon.

This house seems to relate intimately to the land around it, as does Gladys Taber's much older Stillmeadow. I think the people who built a hundred, two hundred or more years back had a feeling for the contours of the land. I've never seen an old house which rose up to smite you in the face. Perhaps it wasn't so much the fancy or design of the builders in those days; perhaps after years upon years a house settles in and becomes a part of the land around it. And the people who live in these houses settle in too and become part of their dwellings. I've always wanted to see for myself where everyone I know lives—and this even includes some people I've never met—so that when I think of them I can visualize their natural surroundings. And sometimes those who have been to visit me for the first time write me thereafter and say, "I'm so glad to know what your house is like, so I can picture you in it."

On the way to the kitchen porch there's a corner broken from a step; this must be mended before winter. Last spring we remedied the cracks in the dining-room ceiling; those which seem daily to appear elsewhere must be patient for a time; and there were bricks in the paths and some of the terrace stones which had heaved. These, too, have been fixed. But the doorstep on the back porch, which you take in rather a long stride—nothing can happen to that. It's one very big, thick stone. I had a friend come once who stooped to touch it with his hand and then said it was going to rain. He explained that where he came from such a stone often predicted weather. I touched it too, and it was slightly damp under my hand. That night it rained.

Once upon a time there were verandas around this house, probably dating from the Civil War, but my predecessors here had them removed. They must have darkened the living room, and possibly the study. In any case they'd been an addition to the original structure. There were other additions before my time here, and I have contributed a few, but all seem to be fitting and to belong.

I walk in the fields, I walk in the woods, I scramble over stone walls and return scratched, sometimes bleeding, and with my stockings in ribbons, wondering if by any terrible chance I have disregarded the poison ivy which, no matter how you fight it, usually wins in the end. It rewards us only with its coloring in autumn, and sometimes even that doesn't reward. I have seen city people driving out to the country on a fine autumn day, leaping from their cars and rushing to tear poison ivy from trees or walls, and leaping back into the cars again, bearing with them what they fondly believe to be decoration. It's always too late to stop them and one shudders to think what condition they and their children—there are always children—will be in before dinnertime in the city.

Curious, isn't it, how many things beautiful in appearance are deadly poison, some to everyone, some only to the allergic? Poison oak, ivy, and sumach, and many lovely berries, to say nothing of toadstools and certain mushrooms. There are many animals lovely to watch but dangerous to be near; and while I am appalled at the tiniest and most harmless snake when it crosses my path, a number of people I know think snakes are beautiful.

I have found in certain fields of art, in literature, in the theater and even occasionally in paintings what, at first reading, hearing, or sight, seems beauty; but a little later proves poisonous to the mind, or spirit—at least, to mine.

Every spring I go to the other side of the pond to look at the little apple tree my younger son and his twin sister planted there before we moved into this house. It was supposed to bear five types of apples. That was a long time ago and only recently has it decided to have even a bud or two. As for apples . . . none, of course. Maybe it didn't want five kinds; maybe it thought five kinds would be confusing and therefore just sat with its roots in the earth and grew a little every year and didn't produce a thing.

If I'm right, it's being very sensible, for if you are confused, or believe you will be, what you produce isn't going to be of much value to you or anyone else.

September

August on Cape Cod produces a pattern of sea gulls. Here, I've none, although I'm not far from the Sound. But those who live on the Sound or any little arm thereof, have sea gulls, and to spare.

Not many minutes away close friends of mine live by the water. They are mother and daughter and I call them my girls. There are shrubs, roses, and hedges about the house, and they've gardens of vegetables and flowers and, likewise, fruit trees. The lawn goes down to a sea wall and to a dock. You walk out on the dock and, if you desire to swim when the tide is right, descend a ladder (having, I hope, put on your bathing suit). There's land to be seen and little points of it run water-ward. I think there's an island or two. And when the fog rolls in, there's a fog horn blowing in its oddly melodic, however harsh, manner.

All manner of boats go by and many sea gulls come in to sit on the dock or the sea wall and even invade the bird bath. My girls feed them, but most of all they feed a large, belligerent, aggressive, clever sea gull whose name is Birdock.

Few people have ever known a sea gull named Birdock, but my girls do, and hence, I do too. He has for years taken up his post on the dock or sea wall, so they have come to distinguish him from all others. When they put out food—any food, for sea gulls are natural scavengers—there he is, making loud, defensive noises, fighting off any other gull who eagerly flies in. I think he always wins.

Last winter—it was, I think, February—my girls and I had mid-day dinner at a hotel, and looking at the remains of my prime roast beef, a large untouched piece and the rib, I said, "I wish you had a dog."

Said they to me, "We'll take it home and give it to Birdock."

I was stunned, but willing. I asked our waitress for a proper bag to accommodate pets. I couldn't bring myself to say, "for a sea gull." But later I thought I'd give her something to think about. "Actually," I admitted, "the beef is for a sea gull." She fell back, aghast, and I visualized her calling the nearest mental hospital. But I heard her laughing as we left.

Back we went and put the meat and the rib on the lawn. Birdock flew down at once, swallowed the beef whole, took the rib to the top of the sea wall, and proceeded to pick at it. In came half a dozen gulls. Birdock screamed. They went away, except one or two more valiant and hungry gentlemen or ladies, but they, too, were soon vanquished.

I finally ceased to watch. I couldn't stand seeing Birdock, without benefit of hands, attacking that rib. Later I was told that he flew off with it; maybe he dropped it in the water. I can't imagine that he buried it.

As for his name, my girls have a small-boy neighbor. He, too, became interested in this faithfully recurrent gull and out of the two words, "bird" and "dock," fashioned Birdock.

I am very happy to know, even slightly, a sea gull, large, proud, always hungry, extremely hostile to interference, and with so interesting a name. I used to apply it only to an equally aggressive weed, differently spelled.

I'm not sure whether Birdock's a year-round guest or whether he comes only in special seasons. If he's there this month, I think I'll go out and buy him a pound of the best hamburger.

This is the pleasant month when it can be very hot by day—

think of Labor Days in this section, for example—hotter than July and cool by night. Many people who do not have school-age children take vacations in September. For two or three years I was fortunate in that I could remain on the Cape half of September A couple of years ago I returned on the day after Labor Day, and the long drive, the incredible traffic, and the fact that the temperature was over 90, still fills me with retrospective horror. But there were rewards; for instance the perfectly wonderful man who helped us when we broke down just beyond the main street in Providence. He pushed us a long, long way and when we tried to repay him, said, "I like to help people in trouble. Makes me believe that sometime, when I'm in trouble, someone will help me."

That's pretty sound philosophy.

The friend who drove me and I spent considerable time at the gas station to which we'd been pushed by the Good Samaritan and then went on for quite a while before we found a place open for luncheon. But we did eventually, and it was spacious, cool, uncrowded, and named, of all things, "Yellow Jacket."

As the leaves redden and the winds cool the nights laced with stars, as apples ripen on the bough and birds gather in large conventions—as vocal as any political conventions, I daresay—to discuss their plans for going south, we travel into another autumn, taking with us our personal luggage: the things we remember, and those to which we look forward. And, of course, we carry with us—because we haven't sense enough not to—old anxieties and apprehensions as well as the new. It's a good thing that we aren't flying on real airplanes, for the overweight would be terribly expensive. In addition to our personal fears we pack the world's tensions and fears, though we know that in every generation there's been the veiled face of the future and a troubling of the waters. Those of us who express terror add to the world misery, for one of the most contagious things, negatively speaking, is fear. It spreads like an epidemic. There are other thought forces equally contagious, but these are more rare; courage is one; optimism another; and above all, faith.

For fear, as this autumn comes, I'd like to substitute compassion—not pity—but the true empathy one feels for another's grief or desperation; compassion, too, for those who have died, or will die, by violence; for the gnawing hunger of millions of children; for the hopelessness and loneliness of the old, who find themselves alone and forgotten; and for illness, pain, and suffering the world round. I honestly believe that compassion has a healing quality, for it is love, however impersonal, and it is also prayer, however silent.

Walking down this September road, which is beginning to show its true colors and which leads, wonderfully into new activities and old ones reassumed, I try to remember that there is always the day we call tomorrow, no matter what it will bring to the world, to those I love, to those I have never known, and to me. Always tomorrow; and if it does not dawn here, then elsewhere, life being eternal. I am not, for myself, afraid of the future. In some ways I do fear it, for my children and their children. But as I've tried to say before, the future never really comes, it is always ahead of us, around the road's next bend; the past lies behind us, recreated only in thought and memory, sometimes happily and sometimes not. It is in today that we actually live, in the present, the immediate moment, the Now. And I think that we were meant to make the best, and the most, of it; this hour, this very moment.

William Cowper has said, "God moves in a mysterious way His wonders to perform." None among us, however contemplative, however brilliant, can solve the mystery of His way—although many have tried, from the mystics to the skeptics—and few of us, in our hearts, question it. We can only think about it with humility as we live one day at a time and take one step at a time, in spiritual confidence as nearly as we can achieve it. I have learned long since, the hard way, that the fortress is within. I have spoken of it as a lighthouse, a citadel, a beacon. It doesn't matter by what symbology you arrive at a description of your personal inner security; it is important that it be there whatever you call it. You cannot find it in a book, although you can read about it;

125

you cannot derive it from a sermon, however beautiful, or from the counsel of wise men. Oh, you can read, and listen, but what you read and hear are merely words, however valid and stirring. The answer lies within ourselves, within you, within me, for trust is part of one's self. You can say, over and over, "I trust." But saying doesn't make it so; it has to *be* so. To this fortress we can at any time retreat, each after his own fashion. This is not a refusal to face reality, it is simply a going home.

I have not always known this, except with my mind, which accepted it years ago. Now I know it, apart from my mind; I know it through experience. Belief is one thing; most of us believe in something, but belief is easily shaken. Experience is deeply personal, it is private, and the trust and faith born of experience cannot be shaken, at least not fatally and never for long. It is difficult to share experience with others; you may try to do it in words, but there is always something lacking. You can say, "Look, this happened to me; this I believe," and your friend may, or may not, accept what you say. But until he himself has experienced, in his own way, what you have felt and experienced, he cannot grasp it beyond the ordinary meaning of the spoken word.

In this season, a steppingstone between summer and true autumn, the wild ducks come calling as they do also in the spring. There is deep water in the little brook-fed pond only when we've had good heavy rains. When first we came here to live we had a pair of mallards with us all year, except when the pond was frozen; there was enough natural food in it to sustain them, and if a strange duck flew in, they rose up and attacked him. If they didn't succeed in driving him away, they'd waddle solemnly up the long slope side by side and sit patiently on the edge of the millstone birdbath until the uninvited guest decided to depart. I have, several times in the past, encountered my mallards walking up the brick path.

But in recent years a school has been built not far away, houses have gone up with dogs in residence. Things are growing crowded even for the wild ducks. Now and then I see them flying—and their flight is very lovely—across an evening sky; occasionally they pause, come to rest in the pond, and then take off again. For them it must be as it is for us when we return briefly to look at a place in which we once lived, undisturbed and happy, but from which we have been forced by circumstances to move.

I'm happy that sporadically they do come back, to quack to one another about the old days. They know that the pond will always be there . . . well, perhaps not, for it has made a sort of tunnel for itself and nowadays never quite fills up but runs underground like a person's secret thoughts. The ducks, however, know that when there's water, there is sustenance, so they stop by, as you might go to see an old neighbor, hoping for a slice of pound-cake and a cup of China tea. I always feel a vivid flash of joy when I see them return for a little stopover. In the early years here, I took them for granted. Now when they come, it's a bonus.

A year ago last March I went walking on a beach with my daughter-in-law in St. Augustine, where I'd not been before. We had driven out to see the Marineland there, and the gay, laughing dolphins—natural show-offs, perfect clowns, and wonderful friends. On the way back to our motel outside the city, we went for a beach walk. It was sunny, cool, and windy on the ocean and as we fore-sook the rough path for the hard white sand, we found lying there, the wings outspread, a snow goose, that most beautiful bird, only recently dead. I had never seen one before, but I thought I recognized the species and looked it up when I returned home. Apparently he was off course; he wasn't supposed to be where his white, black-tipped wings had carried him. I do not know how he died, though seemingly it was not by violence. However it was, he had lost his way.

So we go off course, all of us, now and again, and when we do, something of beauty and of value dies.

This is the month when the stars blaze and we can go outdoors, take a deep breath, and look ahead. It doesn't matter that we cannot see far, either by day or night. All comers hold mystery. Beyond a turn we often come upon it unexpectedly.

I do hope that the mallards will return this month or next, if only for half an hour. Alas, they are not as fortunate as Birdock, who is quite aware that the wide blue salt water remains, the dock stands and the sea wall; and even if my girls are off on a trip—as they were last spring and summer—there will be a neighbor or someone to feed him. He can even forage for himself, although he's very spoiled. But self-preservation is a great spur. I suppose, while his involuntary hostesses were absent, Birdock must often have sat on the dock or wall, his head between his shoulders, thoughtfully hunched there, perhaps watching for an unwary fish and wondering where the people had gone who lived in the big white house, and who had for so long provided him with nourishment. It wasn't the first time they'd traveled away on big ships in whose wakes there are usually gulls. I think each time they saw a gull they must have thought of Birdock, brooding upon the injustice of life but muddling through until they came home again.

The really important words of the ten in the familiar William Cowper quotation given above are, "God moves." And so He does. He moves through the wind, no matter from what direction it may blow. He moves through the dazzling sky or the dark; through the whipped-cream clouds or the thunderheads. He moves with each of us upon our personal roads. He reddens the apple and the leaf, shines in the star and the waning and waxing moon. He moves in every blaze of sunlight, every drop of rain, and in all storm. And knowing that He moves with us, and within the world, we need not fear also to move, as He wills us, which is, I believe, always forward.

Everything moves, the swift-flying birds, the creeping reptile, the animal, the insect, the worm, the plodding snail, the turtle, the butterfly. Rocks do, too, although we cannot see their motion, for they have their own mysterious lives. Nothing really stands still: not the earth beneath us, however solid it may feel except when torn by tremors, or the sky above us. Why should we stand still, hesitant, and fearing the next step?

All water moves: the brooks, the rivers, the oceans, the lakes, and ponds. All have a source and all return to the sea. Growth in

128

flower, tree, or shrub is movement. We do not see it, but it is there; even in winter in the ice-locked soil there is the knowledge of spring and of growth.

Children grow. And so do we, long after we have ceased to grow in the physical sense. We reach our normal height and there we remain, until we are old and shrink a little. Sometimes we grow in the wrong direction physically; that's why diets were invented. But always we can grow within ourselves, spiritually; always we can widen the scope of our minds; always we can deepen the good emotions; always we can reach out, in the search for maturity, to share with others their suffering and their joy.

Sometimes it is easier to share another's failure than to rejoice at his success. It's a sign of growing up when we can be whole-hearted in such a rejoicing, without envy, without wondering why couldn't it have happened to us. . . . just feeling pure joy that someone else, friend or stranger, has been made happy by a wide vista of green pastures after, perhaps, a rather narrow and difficult road.

September seems to end one season and to begin another in the cycle of the year. It is somehow magical, to pass from one month to the next, it is also almost imperceptible.

Some fortunate people will go vacationing this month and next, but more of us will return from mountains or shore to resume our busy, preoccupied lives, picking up the threads which were briefly laid aside, and the responsibilities which we never really cast away but which, for a time, we endeavored to forget.

As I walk down the slope, there are a few August apples withered on the ground, rejected by man and woodchuck. The burning bush beside the doorstep has begun to feather out in shocking pink. Migrant birds pause at the feeder or the birdbath and are gone again. I once saw a flock of ruby-crowned kinglets sitting on the branch of the old mulberry tree. They were there only for the space of two or three quickly drawn breaths and then away again. They've never come back, but I'll not forget them. I'll always remember, too, the cedar waxwings, resting in a shrub outside the kitchen of the other house, and gravely passing, one to the other, a little berry. It was a game. The last bird on the branch always dropped the berry to the ground.

Birds play games and so do animals. Have you ever seen bunnies playing leapfrog at dusk? Or young red foxes like fantastic kittens, chasing each other along a stone wall? Or squirrels playing tag?

Last spring, watching the dolphins at their antics—trained by man to be sure, but also naturally amusing themselves through instinct—I had a sudden deep sense of the mysterious ways in which God moves through everything which lives. . . .

Autumn now and, very soon, the month of my birthday coming up—a reminder of the extraordinary struggle I have to make myself believe that I have lived these many years, with, and by faith.

♥§ §♥

"And every common bush afire with God . . ."
ELIZABETH BARRETT BROWNING

The swamp maples turn early and then the dogwood and little by little the other trees follow; leaf by leaf, through all the wine shades, the yellows and oranges of fruit, the berry shades.

A dry summer affects this glory adversely; but when there's been enough benevolent rain, the woods and hills and fields and roadsides explode in such flaming beauty that your instinct is to shade your eyes.

Not all of this is out of doors. I bring in maple branches for instance, careful to cut them where I can trim rather than disfigure, and set them in water in the big floor vases. I also send the best leaves I can find—and that's hard, for insects have done their embroidery upon them earlier in the season—to people who, living in another country or climate, are homesick for autumnal color. My daughter-in-law in Florida always asks for leaves for the children to take to school. And she makes little borders of autumn leaves about her windows and so thinks herself back to the Berkshire hills in Massachusetts where she was born. I also send them to friends in England because the trees there do not weave as bright an autumn pattern as here.

I like dried flowers, too, and every September friends give me white and pink hydrangeas. Once upon a time I used to cut the deep blue blossoms from Cape Cod bushes and bring them home with the bayberries. The white hydrangeas become a beautiful pinkish beige, the blue ones fade to amethyst or aquamarine and, as time goes by, they grow so fragile that the least breath of air or even a step upon the floor will send the little blossoms showering down.

Sometimes when the cork bush, or as we call it burning bush, is in full dress, I feel like going outside and putting my face into the branches, to breathe, to drink in, all the variations of pink and red and scarlet. This would avail me nothing but scratches, for the strange flat branches would resent an intruder. They don't seem to mind the birds that fly in and out in every season, especially when the tiny red berries appear.

Now that my birthday approaches I remember that over a year ago I announced that when I was seventy I expected to become very eccentric and to my horror, two of my children who were present asked, simultaneously, "More than *now*?"

I refuse to blame my absent-mindedness on the years because I've always been absent-minded. My father, in exasperation, often called it "mooning." "What's Faith mooning about now?" he'd inquire.

Still, I don't know . . . last night I looked all over the house for a missing shoe and didn't remember until this morning that I'd sent it to the village to be stitched. I also spent some time looking for a card bearing the name of the place where I get these particular shoes. Heaven only knows when and where it will turn up.

In my bedroom on a chest of drawers I have a small enchanting whale made of glass which came to me from the Adirondacks, via France. He is supposed to foretell weather conditions. If they are good, he should be bright cerulean blue; if changing, pink; if wet, lavender. However, he stays blue even if it's pouring outside. I daresay what he really measures is humidity and perhaps he's comfortable in the bedroom. I've never had the heart to put him outside to see if he'd turn color like a chameleon. I always remember the one my parents brought me (a chameleon not a whale) from the Buffalo Exposition. He was on a little gold chain. Someone put him on a table where he turned a simple brown. But someone else put a candlestick over him. So I didn't have him long.

Now and then I stop to consider all the animal facsimiles I appear to have collected, not only the Copenhagen birds and beasts, but marvelous creatures of shell that a friend makes for me, to say nothing of my eagle-on-the-hearth, my brass cat, and the glass whale. There's a glass cat, too, which is also a weather prophet . . . more or less. And last year a young friend gave me a grasshopper of bamboo. Upstairs I have a cricket in a cage . . . and on the small table in the study there's a tall blackbird, I think he's teak and Indian. And almost everywhere there are owls: one painted on the lamp in the sunroom; one made from a coconut and hanging on a door; and a painting of one in the hallway. . . . I am extremely fond of owls. I know why, but I'm not telling.

Now that I consider it, despite my passion for giving things away, I've kept a lot and most of it would bewilder strangers. I can imagine them muttering after they've left, "Why does she like crickets and grasshoppers and owls and dormice and little bears and all kinds of birds?"

Perhaps the only sanity-restoring thing they'd find in the cluster of bric-a-brac, pictures, mugs, and scent bottles scattered all around is the small American flag my neighbors gave me at Christmas for my desk.

I sometimes wonder whether we are attracted to things or things to us!

Now in the bright blue weather before the sun descends and the afterglow of the sunset becomes a reflection of the autumn leaves, before the violet dusk comes down and the stars look out, I think

I'll put on a tweed coat and go walking down the road a little way —not far, being lazy and hating exercise—but just in order to breathe the quiet fresh air and watch the trees cool off as darkness nears.

October

This is the month in which, early, I wrote many thank-you letters. The fact that my handwriting is illegible, even to me, does not deter me. My mother was a tartar when it came to thank-you notes in return for presents, for dinner parties, for anything at all; she also made me a compulsive note writer. When friends are away on long trips, I bombard them daily, using the oddest, longest addresses (and get half the mail back months later). When anyone gets engaged or married whose grandmother or great-grandmother has even passed through my backyard, I write. And I answer my own mail so promptly that the recipients go into declines. But there's a reason. If I don't it would pile up and I'd never get at it.

My mother didn't approve of typewritten thank yous. She ignored my handwriting (hers was clear and pretty, my father's beautiful) and I'm sure she also ignored my typing. That's even worse than the penmanship.

Anyway this is the one month, which on the first, brings me something different!

This month I'm seventy-one. Last year on my birthday I startled friends who were with me for dinner by announcing solemnly that

I'd reached the Biblical fourscore and ten. "Ah," said one guest, "you have your Bible confused with the Gettysburg speech!"

I did some mental finger counting and came up with the answer. I wasn't ninety; I was seventy.

All this past year I haven't quite believed it except when I looked in the mirror at night after a busy day or in the early morning. Then I saw double.

If, however, we counted as the Chinese do, I'd be a year older than I am.

I shall hate to see this month depart, the banners of flame flicker out, the gold and scarlet glory dim. I shall not like having to turn the clock back to sun-time and watching the days darken early. The only consolation is that after December twenty-first, the year's shortest day, they'll lengthen again. You hardly notice it until, say, February. Nor do you notice in June, that after the longest day, they begin to shorten.

Warm days now, sometimes; cool nights; and often autumnal rains. October often has an April quality about it, and I find myself listening for the silver chorus of peepers, looking for a young green shoot in the long-since-put-to-bed garden, and thinking about the silent mole and his lethal way with bulbs.

October is a good month in which to remember her opposite number, April, and for thinking about the summer past. Florida, Long Island, the Cape—beaches and sand dunes. I like to project myself backward or considerably forward and purposely skip thinking about winter, for we have had some shuddery ones—windy, bitter cold, and trimmed with ice as well as snow.

There are tropical and semitropical climates where the alteration of seasons is barely perceptible. Changes as a rule mean a rainy season. I often remember the Rain-maker, the flat-topped mountain that you see as you come into Pago Pago. If you look at the clouds it wears, they'll tell you if it is going to rain. When I was there, it did, most of the time.

Well, tropical and semitropical climates are wonderful, and fun to inhabit for a little while, but I'd not like to remain in any of them year-round. Though I have often said I dislike change, but try to adjust to it, this does not apply to the seasons. I like variety in the seasons even when one afflicts me—such as a too-hot summer, or a too-cold winter. In the cycles of this particular climate the changes are slow yet sometimes seem sudden: the first faint mist of green along the bough; the little violet leaf beneath the covering of dry, brown leaves; the first leaf that blushes on the cork bush; the first red signal of the swamp maple; the first snow-flake or glitter of ice on the birdbath. And, of course, the first migrant bird in autumn and the first spring bird which soars to the feeder.

I believe that seasonal changes stimulate; at least there is nothing monotonous about them. Certainly in my neck of the woods we complain, and loudly, that winter lasts far too long, but we are sensible enough to know that it cannot last forever. Nothing does except the basic qualities upon which our lives are, or should be, founded; and these are all the myriad expressions of love, personal and impersonal, which reflect the love of God for all His creations.

Along the year's road that we walk there are always enchanting vistas. Now, with that gypsy month October, we walk toward Thanksgiving, then toward Christmas and the New Year, and after that, we are slipping, sometimes quite literally, toward spring and summer.

Each season brings its astonishments and its rewards and inevitably, in our personal lives, sorrows and happiness, worries and problems. Sometimes, when I lament—and I do very often—that I'm tired of crisis following crisis, someone says, "Well, never a dull moment!" To which I respond without gratitude, "No, but I wish there were!"

Never a dull moment isn't strictly true for anyone. We all have dull moments and usually resent them instead of welcoming them. We are restless, or bored, or just feel flat, all the fizz gone. However they do provide a respite, a breathing spell. While I daresay a life unimperiled by crisis, untouched by grief, unshaken by anxiety, would be remarkably easy (actually, I cannot believe such a life really exists), it would—like the climate which never alters—become tedious.

As the body learns to adapt to changing conditions—the drop, or rise, in temperature; the sudden, unseasonable thaw or freeze—so the intelligence and emotions must learn to adjust to altering circumstances, to endure the sudden blow, or the seemingly endless anxiety.

It is not from the easy path that we learn our lessons, but from the hard one. Only at intervals is the road level; mostly it is uphill. I have discovered, however, that once you have climbed a hill, the view from the top is marvelous. You look back and down and wonder how you ever accomplished that ascent. Other hills may, and probably do, lie before you, but at least this one has been conquered. There's a descent and then another uphill path, but possibly somewhere in between, a little plateau on which one may walk awhile, gathering inner strength before attempting the next hard climb.

Someone I love very much said to me not long ago, "I see you are still carrying the burdens." Well, who doesn't? Little ones, light as feathers; middle-sized ones, or heavy. Maybe a few people do not have any of these, but it is comforting to know oneself to be among the vast majority.

All burdens shift; some are laid aside; others take their places and sometimes, particularly as one grows older and less resilient, seem heavier. For, as time passes, elasticity and rebound are reduced and it becomes more difficult to meet the challenge.

For years I've been talking and writing, in private and in public, about the necessity of taking life one step at a time. Few, I find, do. And I do not practice what I preach—at any rate, not every day. I still look ahead, to visualize and dread disasters which may never happen. Perhaps the best thing we can all do is to ask for that one step, and only one, and for the strength to take it and then go on from there.

I consider this month, as I always have, the start of a personal new year. Looking back I find that the bounties and deprivations of the year just passed have been about equal. There have been times when I've refused to count my blessings, but I know I must.

October brings with her unique gifts which are peculiarly her own. The gypsy bandana confining her wild red hair is of every hue; all the colors of sunrise and sunset and of the sun itself. She will blow warm and cold; she will bring straight downpouring, or free-blowing, rain to soak into the ground and fill the brooks and sometimes flood their banks and she will, as always, bring to me an exciting gaiety and an expectation. When October first dawns, I always think: Let this gypsy cross my palm with gold.

Few of us admit that our pathway is easy. There are always obstacles, expected or unexpected, which bring us to a complete halt as we wonder how we can surmount them. Always the turns, the high hills, the downward going and the flat, monotonous stretches. Often there is darkness. I daresay all of us pray, as Goethe did, for more light; light upon the personal path; enough, at least, for that one step forward.

Actually, as I keep telling myself, the light is always there, but we stand in the way. Human beings cast very long shadows and walk in them. All of us know that we cast the shadows of self from the time we become conscious of being alive until we are no longer living in this small special world; shadows, too, of vanity, resentment, and envy; shadows of sorrow and regret; frustration and insecurity.

We can, I think, through conscious endeavor, shorten the self-shadows and lengthen the light. It isn't easy. Everything worth while takes time and unremitting work. An artist, whether in paint, or music, or words, does not just "toss off" that which he tries to create. A good actor, during his every performance, tries to achieve perfection and to bring a new freshness to a role many times repeated. A dancer practices between appearances. A sound business is built upon work and worry, and is, at its best, an example of true craftsmanship. Any singer worth his salt studies for many years and keeps on studying after he has reached the pinnacle of success. The doctor, the nurse, the lawyer, the teacher cannot afford to rest upon the laurels won at graduation. No one can. As for the seemingly less exciting occupations, no one was born knowing how to cook, clean, sew, wood carve, or garden.

They have to learn. I wish I'd been born to do many things I cannot, but it's too late now.

I've learned a few things as I've walked, run, or stumbled along my road—theoretically, at least. I know very well that fear and worry are destructive forces, as are all negative thoughts. This is all as true as sunrise, but the knowledge hasn't kept me from fear or worry or negative thinking. I also know that envy is as bad for us as a dose of poison. I've said for years that I envy no one, and it isn't strictly true, or not all the time. I've envied people—a great many of them—who are better writers than I. Sometimes I learn of something which has happened, magically, to another and feel a pang. We all do. When something tragic comes our way, we ask: Why to me? When something wonderful happens to someone else, we inquire: Why *not* me?

Well, perhaps it's because we haven't the talent, or the rich Uncle from Down Under. Usually the person to whom something marvelous happens has earned it in one way or another, and tragedy comes to everyone.

If you've spent five, ten, twenty, or more years of your life planning and working and the completion of your work covers you with glory, then you've earned it. But envy is a very common, thoughtless, and wholly human trait. I try to remember when, briefly, I envy someone something they have earned that the laborer is worthy of his hire.

I've always wanted to do more than I can and much for which I have not the talent. There are places I long to see and have never seen and probably never will. There are things I've wanted to do and be, and have not done nor become. In this, as in many other things, I'm a lot like everyone else.

October is a corridor of gold and flame as we walk down it toward the darker months and winter. Normally in this section of the world October is a blaze of glory, but that doesn't happen without work either; for nature, too, works at her job.

During this month I'll take my friend Agnes to look at the dogwood which grows in such profusion all around us and particularly

139

in one section. Every spring we drive through the incredible, enchanting maze of flowering trees, pink, deeper pink, and every shade of white from ivory to flesh-colored. But people forget how beautiful the trees are in autumn, the flowers gone, the leaves darkly maroon and the red berries clustered thickly on the branches. It's a very good idea to get there before the birds do, however, for dogwood berries are as delightful to their taste as to our sight.

At the end of this month children from neighboring homes will come crowding to our doors in their funny little costumes, demanding "Trick or Treat." I remember one year when a child came who was small enough to wear just a pillow case, with holes cut in for eyes, nose and mouth. "What exactly does he represent?" I asked the older child with him—or her—and the older child replied, "Just a ghost!"

I strip the little foyer of the breakables and Gussie brings me lollipops and candy and all the things children like. I also keep small change at hand for the boxes in which they collect money for less fortunate youngsters. So when they knock at the door I fill their bags with all manner of sweet if sometimes indigestible goodies, and if they have the official boxes along, I drop in the coins.

Now that I think of it, life knocks at one's door very often, saying, "Trick or treat?" For living demands that you give something to it; if you do not, then, through your own fault of short sight or sheer stubbornness, you are vulnerable to the trick.

I am always asked, long before my birthday, what I want. I can think now of at least a hundred quite impossible things, which remind me of Alice in Wonderland (and also Through the Looking Glass) and of the White Queen who could believe six impossible things before breakfast. There's a great deal of wisdom in the ageless *Alice*. I hope you remember her and also the Red Queen, who reasonably contended that it took all the running you could do to stay in one place and therefore at least twice as much to get anywhere else.

So what do I want for my birthday? All the one hundred impossible things, I suppose, which, rolled into one, would be peace of mind. We all want that, I'm sure; and I'll try this year to believe, before every breakfast, that it isn't impossible.

I also want other things which can't be wrapped in pretty paper or tied with gay ribbons or sent through the mail. Patience for one, courage for another, and understanding. I think that, most of all, I desire understanding, even just a little, of other people, of myself, of what living entails, demands, and offers, and of the pattern which every day I create. It is flawed as are most patterns; sometimes gay, sometimes threaded with gold, sometimes drab and dark, often a little soiled, but always discernibly, if I can but understand it, a pattern.

I stopped writing just now in order to indulge myself in a brief moment of irritation. I had asked to be brought some medium-soft pencils already sharpened. They have arrived, but they are not sharpened. They are sitting here looking at me, as blunt as a criticism. Oh, well, a friend recently fixed my sharpener for me (it had grown tired), so I'll sharpen them myself, every one. For I have to do a—to me—unpleasant job which requires figures, columns, additions, and subtractions, and I never got an A in mathematics, not even the most simple. All this requires good sharp pencils and lots of them.

You know, small things can be gadflies. Larger matters are wasps and may sting you to death, or nearly so, if you are allergic. But the little things irritate like gnats.

Most of us seem able to meet the big crises, even head on. We get up, bruised and even bleeding, from the ground to which we've been flung, and go on somehow. But the little things throw us like restive horses which we haven't learned to ride.

Sitting here alone in the study, with the night crowding in at the windows, past the drawn pink shades and brown curtains, I find myself laughing a little at small irritations, all of which pass so quickly. Perhaps they are good for us.

But I am a person who, for instance, would be resigned to pneumonia, antibiotics, and the oxygen tent; at least I'd feel somewhat important. I despise the common cold, however. It runs its course and you get over it, but it's an annoyance. It hampers, it deters, it keeps you for a short time from doing what you feel you must do. To serious illness you adjust; there's nothing you can do about it, so you let the doctors, nurses, and your family worry. But who sympathizes with a cold in the head?

See, the major things are managed somehow but the minor irritations seem unmanageable.

I may, on a winter's night, have a speaking engagement. What I have to say is not important. If I don't get there, no one will suffer. Yet I struggle over terrible roads or flounder in the snow and slip on the ice with the firm conviction that, if I don't get to where I'm supposed to be at that very moment, the world will end.

Well, it won't; not for me, not for the potential audience, most of whom won't get there either, but will wisely spend a cosy snowbound evening at home, reading, sewing, or watching television.

If, on the other hand, on an equally frustrating night I should be trying to get to someone I love who needed me, I wouldn't notice the ice or the snow or the skids. . . .

Minor; major; this is the way the music of living is played; these are the chords one strikes, with small, happy melodies in between.

So now, having celebrated my seventy-first birthday, I embark on another year, during which, on each of the other three hundred and sixty-four days I may, as Humpty Dumpty said to Alice, have an unbirthday present.

⤚§ ৡ⤙

"I'll not go back to the cruel gray street
To the cold, gray city skies.
I'll build my house where the wind runs free;
And the stars have friendly eyes."

There's more to the above poem; two more verses in fact, each of them pretty bad. I don't think you'll find it in any anthology. It's one I wrote myself a good many years ago. I don't remember when. I don't think it is in my first book of verse, of which I haven't a copy; and I know it isn't in the second.

Well, let's take it apart. I must have been living in the city and whatever street I lived on, while it may have been gray, certainly wasn't cruel. And the skies over a city, if somewhat obscured by smoke, smog, and the like, are the same skies which arch above the countryside (those can also be gray). The wind runs free in a city too; it just has to get around houses; and the stars, I'm sure, are friendly everywhere.

I happen to have a copy of these verses only because my father had a wonderful half sister. Aunt Jo was often with us, and in our city house, somewhere along the line I must have perpetrated these verses. She liked them and had a great many copies printed, "suitable for framing," if anyone wished. I framed none; I did give a number away. A few remain in a drawer of the living-room desk here.

Another verse says "I'll build my house where love abides." Well, I've never built a house, but I go along with love in whatever house I inhabit. Then I speak of gates swinging open. There has never been a gate anywhere I've lived, so we'll think of that as metaphoric. The verse also mentions a path worn by friendly feet. Here, I have two paths; they are brick and what wears them down is not feet but ice, snow, and rain!

Apparently I thought a path should be bordered by shy, hiding-away wild flowers. . . . No self-respecting wild flower would hide around any of these paths, except in the grass beyond the violets.

In the last verse I announce that I'll be surrounded by my books, and that's true enough; wherever I've gone, there have been books. I also add "my songs," and this is sheer poetic license: I cannot carry a tune; I don't own a piano and haven't for some years had a record player. There is always, of course, the possibility that someone else is singing around here on television or radio.

Toward the end I speak of a great oak tree that bends to wind

143

and rain. Well, I have oak trees on this property, but oaks don't bend much. I also add that I'll take my peace with my friends, and that's valid enough. . . .

As I can't remember when this was written, I can't tell whether it was mere fancy or the halting expression of a dream.

But when I came across this, I was looking for a quotation pertaining to houses and I'd run out of them. . . . I'd feel happier if I could quote something from my first book of verse, which was about old houses. But I haven't the book and the copy I've asked the out-of-print people to look for hasn't materialized out of someones attic.

Well, whatever I was thinking, planning, or dreaming back in those long past days appears in substance to have come true.

This happens more often than we think; we have a wish, a dream, a desire, and in the course of the years it comes true; perhaps not quite as we had originally pictured it, perhaps it bears only a faint resemblance to the original dream, but the spirit, the essence, is there.

Someone wrote me the other day from a distant state, asking what our winters are like. Having been briefly in this section, she longed for a house in New England, but thought she was too old to realize her dream. Actually in my opinion, colored of course by my considerable seniority, I don't think she's too old, and I hope she sees her dream become reality. Perhaps she won't pull up stakes and pioneer in this district; but maybe she'll have her house sometime, but elsewhere. I hope so. And I hope, too, that wherever she goes, she will find contentment. If she doesn't move from her present home, she might even discover that all she's wished for is right there if only she'd look about her.

So often we think if we could just be somewhere else everything would come up roses. We're restless, we're dissatisfied, and the grass is greener on the other side of the fence. A good many things are factors in the urge to move on: boredom, monotony, the ingrained human belief that anywhere but where you are is a better place. So, if circumstances allow, pull up your roots and plant them elsewhere. Sometimes they take firm hold; sometimes they do not;

144

sometimes there's disappointment and often, a sort of nostalgia.

One thing I know for certain and that is wherever you go, be it to a neighboring state, across the country or the oceans, even to the ends of the earth—which aren't as far away as once they were —you take yourself with you. Nothing essentially changes in you, only in what you see around you.

Now, I think I'll have a look at a month about which I cannot write from knowledge. Oh, I've known a great many Novembers, each a trifle different from the others; but this particular one is in the future. So, I'll polish up my crystal ball and see what vision it affords me.

November

I'm taking a leaf from the television program called "That Was the Week That Was," in thinking about the month which, as I write, has not yet been. My insistence on expanding the chronicle of a year into thirteen months mildly astonishes my friends; I think they believe I am trying to promote the often-suggested calendar of thirteen months, each with twenty-eight days.

This isn't so. I just like thirteen and a month which I've not yet experienced can be built up in fancy from memories of other Novembers and wondering what this one will bring.

Last year, on Thanksgiving Day, I was with close friends in their big, remodeled old barn just across the state line. The weather was the very model of a Thanksgiving Day; a little windy, not very cold, with gray skies thinking darkly about snowing when they got around to it, and then sunlight, like the flash of a golden sword, cutting through. Where I'll be this year I do not know. But wherever it is, I'm sure I'll find people I love around me, carving the turkey, cutting the pies, passing the coffee.

I spent many Thanksgivings in the home of my parents—several in the country place at Shelter Island; others in the homes of dear friends; many in my own homes, in the city and in the country;

some in restaurants, made very festive by appropriate decorations; three in countries where Thanksgiving was not a holiday—two in Germany; one in England. And even one in Puerto Rico. But wherever we are on our national holidays, we have the spirit of them with us. . . .

Lately I've been thinking of a friend of my childhood who has long since gone from this world. Her parents were of German descent, although American-born. Her house, which was not far from where I lived, was solid, a little stately, and in it I was—almost always—welcome. I remember the breakfasts with the sun shining in on the fine crystal jar of honey.

Helen and I had a mutual passion for potato salad and whenever we could beg, borrow or steal a quarter we would skim around to the delicatessen and bear home, to her house, a soggy little container—square in those days. This we would secrete in the upstairs room we shared on the occasions when I was permitted to spend the night. We would also filch cold tea, in milk bottles, from the refrigerator and find two tumblers. When we retired, we took a kitchen saucer and a thick candle, which we lighted, and then affixed to the saucer, feeling that the small flame would not be noticed, whereas if we lit the gas, it would be.

Why we didn't die of overeating, I don't know. But there was never such potato salad anywhere—not even in Germany where, in later years, I ate it . . . the thin-sliced waxy potatoes, the dressing sharp with onion and vinegar. We must have had remarkable digestions, as we washed it down with cold tea.

Unfortunately, Helen's mother loathed onions, and she could scent one a mile off; we would come to breakfast, she would sniff a time or two, and then I'd be sent home. I was always being sent home, and when Helen came to my house we fell into other mischief, she was sent home, too.

I remember one occasion, and it must have been in early winter, perhaps November, when we decided we were tired of our daily routine and thought that possibly a long, serious illness, one which would cause our families to regret their various unkindnesses and injustices, was indicated. Pneumonia seemed a good idea at the time. There was a vacant lot nearby—or perhaps it was a playground—I've forgotten. Thither we repaired, bundled up against wet weather, for it had snowed and then rained. Anyway, we took off our rubbers and went happily wading through icy puddles for a considerable length of time. Then we put the rubbers on again and departed, each to her own house, to await the onset of the disease, the solicitude, the family doctor, the fetch and carry and spoiling of bedside nursing.

We didn't catch so much as a slight cold.

I am thankful for all funny little memories, without importance except as part of the pattern. Every now and then, when I eat potato salad, I think of the house with the sunny dining room, the German mottoes on the walls and Helen's mother crying, "Girls, come her this instant! Closer!" And I doubt that nowadays I would be comfortable with that curious bedtime snack eaten by flickering candlelight.

We are all grateful for the big memories, the remembrance of happiness, of places once visited in which we have known delight. We are all grateful for the truly important recollections—first love, graduation, a wedding day, the birth of a child, the memory of a beginning friendship which was to last lifelong. We are grateful when we remember first success and our first spiritual awareness. But we should, I believe, be equally thankful for the small things, gay, humorous and tender which have come to us like small gift-wrapped surprises along the way.

It is said that everything we have seen, done, experienced, felt, read, and assimilated, is in our subconscious minds. Most of us know this is true when a scent, a view, a word, or a song brings back things we thought long since forgotten.

A great many years ago I was with my father in a car, riding over country roads, when what I can only designate as a country odor—a very strong one—assailed us. My father twitched his nose and said something in Chinese.

Now he had left China when he was eleven years old and as fluent in Chinese as in English. As time went on, however, he

went to school in the states and he lost the other language . . .
actually the first one he'd learned. He was sensitive about having
been born in China because the other children teased him. If I'd
asked him to say three Chinese words of his own accord, I doubt
that he could have done so. But that day he did and was amazed
when I said, "You spoke Chinese." He had not realized it. The
words—and I'll never know what they were—were spoken from his
subconscious.

I wish I knew how to draw on mine. I can sometimes, deliber-
ately, usually just before I fall asleep. All day perhaps I've been
trying to remember a name, or an address, or possibly where I've
put something which I haven't been able to find. So I say to my
subconscious: What was it? Or: Where is it? And nine times out
of ten I wake up remembering. It's the same with time. I do not
rely on my subconscious to tell me I have to get up at, say, seven.
I have an ace in the hole—a small alarm clock—but I usually wake
up just before it rings.

I'd like so much to be able always to tap this reservoir of memory
at will, to be able to recall a hundred thousand things my conscious mind has forgotten: episodes, vistas, passages from books
I've loved and no longer possess. But I do not know how.

Now I am remembering last Thanksgiving, gratefully, and when
this next one comes I'll build myself another little cache of remem-
brances to take with me through the rest of this year and into the
next.

At this season it would be quite wonderful to remember everything for which I've been grateful all my life from the first time
I was conscious of myself as a person, or my parents, and those
around me.

But alas, in common with so many other people, I find I don't
remember what I had for dinner last night—not that that's vital—
or the name of someone I met last week and re-encountered on
the street today.

Those who believe in reincarnation say that under hypnosis or
through a flashback of ancient memory people can recall parts of

149

some of their past lives, indeed, even all of them. And I know many persons who have often had the firm conviction on entering a house, a village, a city, or a country for the first time that they had been there before. This sensation has never been mine. I'd like it, if it were.

Anyway, memory, conscious, subconscious, or atavistic is important. And memory loss is strange and disturbing.

Now, in November, when the road is sometimes muddy, sometimes flecked with early snow, and the stubborn pink-brown leaves are still clinging to the oaks, we climb the little hill to Thanksgiving and then coast down it, very swiftly, to Christmas. And, in dreaming forward like this, I find myself projected back into time, back into early autumn, summer, and spring, even back into last winter, and so around to the reminder that another cold, cold one lies ahead.

Time is rather like an accordion; you can squeeze it until it folds, one month upon the other, or stretch it out to its fullest length, and there are the months, one after another.

Just for this moment, I am suspended in time, ceasing to go forward or back, but idle, willing the moment to stay longer than it was meant to remain.

The friend to whom this book is dedicated has shared a great many memories with me. We were girls together and I remember her house, and she, mine; and we remember each other's parents and friends we had in common. We remember schooldays and vacations. I used to visit her on Long Island, and she would visit me. Now and then when we are together in these later years, a memory pops up in her mind or mine, and we ask each other, "Do you remember . . . ?"

That's one of the very pleasant things about friendship, about any close relationship, the do-you-remember moments.

I wonder if she remembers the time a boy we both knew went sleepwalking on the roof of the Inn where he and his family were staying and where I was visiting Janet. It caused quite a furor as he had been sleeping in the raw. He was right at the roof's edge when someone looked out of a window and saw him, but dared not scream lest he go right on walking over the edge.

In this workroom are the books I've written, in various editions, and some in other languages (which I can't read) and every time I finish a book—as I'm doing right now—I wonder if there will ever be another. There always has been since the first one was published in 1921. A lot of books and far too many words. I don't remember the earlier ones. Sometimes, when they are reprinted I look at them, once or twice I've even read one and wondered how the story would end, for actually I'd forgotten.

A lifetime spent with words is strange. All you have before you is a typewriter (in my next incarnation I must really learn to type properly, or perhaps by then we'll just talk to a machine and I don't mean a dictaphone) and white or yellow paper and sheets of carbon and erasers and pencils with which to correct, after a fashion, the many errors. But to paint! Now there's a beautiful medium, all colors. Or to be able to play a musical instrument and fashion lovely sound. The clatter of a typewriter has no beauty and even if you use a colored ribbon (Gladys Taber likes green ribbons and green ink), it cannot be at all like putting color-filled brush to canvas.

I've known people with several talents . . . Ted Key not only paints and draws, but writes. My friend Elsie Janis could write; she could create both songs and music; she could dance, sing, and act. Many have multiple talents, but they all spring from the same source.

I can't even sew. I tried the other night to sew snap fasteners on the skirt of a suit. I was going to wear it to church and it occurred to me that if I took a deep breath and stood up with a hymnbook my skirt would not rise obediently with me. It has become almost impossible for me to thread a needle, even when I'm wearing glasses, but I found a packet of crewel-work needles in the drawer of my mother's old lampstand. They are wonderful. They have large, and to me, beautiful eyes; and they are not very thick needles at all; just right. So, laboriously, sometimes forgetting to make a knot in the thread, I sewed on those benighted little snaps, which I kept dropping.

In the middle of this labor the telephone rang and it was my old friend Mignon Eberhart. In the course of a conversation about colds and viruses she asked me, what I was doing. I told her; I also told her about the needles, and she remarked that any kind of sewing was, to her mind, crewel work; a pun which I felt was unworthy of her. My son-in-law is passionately addicted to puns. Sometimes he toils over them in order to see my lifted eyebrow and hear my delicate snort. "Don't you think that's funny, Mother?" he asks and I say firmly, "No, I do not." Perhaps I do, really; but it's better not to spoil him.

Now it is time to put this little book—and myself—to bed. Night has fallen as I've been working here and there is just the faintest flush of dark rose lingering, as an afterglow on the edge of the western sky. I just got up and went to the living-room window to see if I could find a star. I could not. I went all over the house, downstairs, and looked. But the dark rose glow is deepening rather than vanishing and after a while I'll look out again and see my star. For there's always one somewhere.

This coming November will have dark nights and starry ones; it will begin its days with sunrise (even if it snows or rains, the sun rises, somewhere); it will end them in sunset and a wash of color across the horizon. But suppose the sun hasn't condescended to shine all day, not even faintly, like a pale yellow sea shell at which you can look without being blinded?

It is there nevertheless, whether we see it or not. And I think the tremendous cause for true thanksgiving is the fact that, as the earth turns according to its orderly plan, and the seasons revolve according to theirs, the stars are always there, as the moon is and the sun, and above all the Creator of all things, by day or night. For there is no time or place in which He is not . . . and so, living by faith, we live in Him.

Happy Thanksgiving.

Finale

". . . the house of my pilgrimage."

PSALM 119: 54

This body is my house, wherein I tarry,
  The view, restricted; the progression, slow;
For, as the snail, my residence I carry,
  Refuge and burden, whereso'ere I go.
I am content; the shelter served me well
  Through what has been, and shall
    through what must be
When I emerge, to leave the outward shell,
  I shall be airborne, soaring light and free.